T0199109

The
COMING BABY
BOOMER CRISIS

The
COMING BABY BOOMER CRISIS

HOW TO PROTECT YOURSELF

DAVID ALMOND, CFP®, MSFS

 iUniverse®

THE COMING BABY BOOMER CRISIS
HOW TO PROTECT YOURSELF

iUniverse books may be ordered through booksellers or by contacting:

iUniverse
1663 Liberty Drive
Bloomington, IN 47403
www.iuniverse.com
1-800-Authors (1-800-288-4677)

Because of the dynamic nature of the Internet, any web addresses or links contained in this book may have changed since publication and may no longer be valid. The views expressed in this work are solely those of the author and do not necessarily reflect the views of the publisher, and the publisher hereby disclaims any responsibility for them.

Any people depicted in stock imagery provided by Getty Images are models, and such images are being used for illustrative purposes only.
Certain stock imagery © Getty Images.

ISBN: 978-1-5320-6036-6 (sc)
ISBN: 978-1-5320-6037-3 (e)

Library of Congress Control Number: 2018912349

Print information available on the last page.

iUniverse rev. date: 12/11/2018

A PRACTICAL HANDS ON GUIDE TO LEARNING:

- Who Pays for Long-Term Care

- How to Protect Yourself from the Two Worries Retirees Have, Running out of Money and the High Cost of Health Care

- How You Can Protect Your Savings and Provide Income Protection for Life

- How to Legally Shelter Your Money Even Without Long-Term Care (LTC) Insurance

- How to Create Tax-Free Income to Pay for Long-Term Care

CONTENTS

ACKNOWLEDGMENTS

Without certain people, this book wouldn't have been possible. My wife, Pam Almond, worked alongside me on many asset-protection cases, always giving great counsel, and is one of the wisest and smartest people I have ever known.

A dear friend and mentor I have worked with for several years, Lisa Bertalan, is an elder-law and estate-planning attorney. She has given me great guidance and has helped shape me as the asset-protection specialist I am today.

Amber (Gouin) Hinds is a friend and asset-protection resource. Amber is second to none as a Medicaid and long-term-care expert. I so much appreciate working with her.

The author is not engaged in rendering legal, tax, accounting, financial planning, investment, or similar professional services. Examples in this book are used for illustrative purposes only and do not represent recommendations or actual results. While legal, tax, accounting, financial planning, and investment issues covered in this book have been checked with sources believed to be reliable, some material may be affected by changes in the laws or in the interpretations of such laws since the manuscript for this book was completed. For that reason, the accuracy and completeness of such information and the opinions based thereon are not guaranteed.

In addition, state or local tax laws or procedural rules may have a material impact on the general recommendations made by the author, and the strategies outlined in this book may not be suitable for every individual. The author encourages the reader to seek professional accounting, legal, tax, financial planning, and/or investment advice before implementing any of the strategies discussed in this book.

INTRODUCTION

"An investment in knowledge pays the best interest."

-Benjamin Franklin

"The heart of the discerning acquires knowledge;
the ears of the wise seek it out."

-Proverbs 18:15

I was referred to help a family where the wife was suffering from dementia. Their caregiver attended the meeting. As I was discussing ways to protect their savings from having to spend it all on care, we got on the subject of asset protection for single people. When the rules changed in 2005 regarding state and federal assistance to pay for long-term care, many thought it was too difficult to help single people save some of their savings. Not true.

The caregiver looked at me, white as a ghost, and said, "David, are you telling me a person can get Medicaid benefits without having to spend down their savings to $2,000?"

I responded, "That is what I am saying."

She explained she had called the state, which is like calling the IRS for tax-planning assistance, and they told her it was necessary to spend down to $2,000, which she did. She was trying to help her disabled father. The wrong information cost her family thousands of dollars.

Unfortunately, there is a lot of misinformation disseminated to the public. Even social workers—bless their hearts—and some senior centers will give the wrong information regarding Medicaid and how to qualify. Sad to say, people who enter a nursing home, on average, will be out of money in eighteen months. Think about the fact that they have spent their working years accumulating their savings that can dissipate rapidly. No wonder long-term care is the number one reason retirees become impoverished.

The two biggest fears retirees have are running out of money and health care. This book will show you how to protect yourself by arming you with the correct information and strategies few people know.

I am writing this book for some important reasons:

1. As in the story I just shared the majority of people don't know how to protect their assets when it comes to health-care. Most retirees fear losing their savings to the high cost of care which doesn't have to happen nor should it.

2. As I mentioned and can't be over stated, there is much misinformation when it comes to asset protection. People are told they have to spend their savings down to $2,000 before they can get Medicaid benefits, *which is not true.* Unfortunately, this misinformation comes from some social workers, senior centers, and state Medicaid offices.

3. With 10,000 Baby Boomers retiring every day there is more stress on Medicaid to help pay for seniors long-term care costs. The majority of people are not aware the government has given us tax incentives to stay financially independent when faced with this expense. I want to share these options with you.

4. How to create income security that can't be outlived providing freedom from stock market volatility. Studies show retirees have more peace of mind when they have guaranteed income and don't have to worry about market volatility.

When I talk about ten thousand baby boomers retiring every day, I think we can all agree growing older comes quickly. I'm reminded of a recent meeting with a client at a restaurant. After having my meal, I excused myself and went to the restroom. As I came out, I told the hostess, who was probably nineteen or twenty years old, "I really like your music." They were playing the seventies' hits, and I am a huge fan of the Eagles, Journey, Foreigner, and other bands of that era. When I am in my car, I crank it up. Truth be told, I am still a kid at heart.

The hostess looked at me without batting an eye and said, "All the old people do."

I said jokingly, "What does that have to do with me?"

I was thinking, *Ouch, that was a little painful*, but the fact of the matter is I actually thought it was pretty funny. It didn't bother me. As the saying goes, growing older is a privilege, and not everyone gets to do it.

I went back to our table and told my client and the server what had happened, and we all had a good laugh. On our way out, the hostess and our server were bussing a table about twenty feet away.

I said, "I need your help."

The hostess replied, "How can I help you?"

I said, "When I came in, I believe you checked in my cane, and now I need it because I have to leave."

Since I don't use a cane, we all had another good laugh. I guess it's like the Nationwide commercial that says, "Life comes at you fast." It sure has.

I said to my client, "I was at the grocery store the other day, and the cashier asked me whether I get the senior discount, which is age sixty or above. I replied to the cashier, not wanting to admit it, 'I guess so.' There was a lady next to me in line, and I said to her, 'It seems like yesterday I was getting carded for beer, and now I'm getting asked whether I get the senior discount. Not sure what happened in between, but I can tell you it was a blink of the eye.'"

These Times Are a Changing

Forty-four years ago, Bob Dylan wrote "These Times They Are a-Changing." As it pertains to our financial well-being, Mr. Dylan's 1964 song rings true today. When it comes to change, there is good news and bad news. The good news is we will probably live longer than at any other time in history; the bad news is we have a greater chance of becoming financially destitute than at any other time in history.

The National Bureau of Economic Research tells us that for millions of retirees, true financial security in retirement will prove an elusive goal. Dr. Ken Dychtwald, the leading authority on aging in America, states in *Age Power* that large numbers of elder boomers could wind up impoverished and that we are woefully unprepared for what is about to occur as our population ages. If that isn't concerning enough, 54 percent of retirees surveyed had never thought about how many years they will spend in retirement, and many are finding out that meeting the financial demands of living longer is proving to be more complicated than they'd envisioned. Moreover, a study conducted by Fidelity Investments tells us that 78 percent of those in retirement do not have a financial plan.

It used to be that a person would expect a relatively short life expectancy after retirement. Now, many of us can plan on one-third of our lives spent in retirement. Today, retirees face a tremendous amount of financial uncertainty. The shift has changed from dying too soon to living too long. Many experts define this longevity risk as the new financial problem.

The new challenge facing retirees today is how to make our money last a lifetime, which leads us to the number one risk to outliving our money, which is the cost of long-term care (LTC). Even though it is the top risk for retirees becoming impoverished, it is the most ignored. Advisers are paid to put together portfolios and investment strategies and crunch the retirement projections, but almost all ignore long-term care. Isn't it logical if we end up with an additional annual expense of $100,000 a year we didn't plan on that our investment portfolio will be turned upside down and our financial security threatened?

The fact is—ignoring this financial landmine is folly. We can't do it and feel safe going into or currently being in retirement. According to the American Health Care Association, "Failure to prepare for the cost of long-term care is the primary cause of impoverishment among the elderly." It is estimated that 58 percent of men and 79 percent of women aged sixty-five and older will need long-term care at some point (*Forbes*). Sadly, only eighteen months after entering a nursing home, many residents are broke. This does not have to be! By knowing how to protect our assets from catastrophic illness, this statistic can—and will—change.

So many families have been affected by Alzheimer's, dementia, and disabilities. I have not been exempt. My personal experience with my father's dementia has motivated me to help others. Over the past eighteen years of specializing in helping people protect their life savings from the high cost of long-term care, I found that the adult children of affected parents are scrambling for direction and answers. Many are getting advice from people who want to assist but are providing information that if acted upon would hurt the family they are trying to help. There is a need for a dependable reference you can turn to for clarity and direction.

The Coming Crisis

Ten thousand baby boomers are retiring every day, and 70 percent will need some form of long-term care during their lifetimes. That number becomes an additional stress on government programs such as Medicare and Medicaid. Medicaid is the leading payer for long-term-care services. The government knows it will be difficult, if not impossible, to sustain the Medicaid program with so many people retiring.

Only about 10 percent of seniors own long-term-care insurance, and that number hasn't changed in the past seven years. Therefore, with the high cost of care, most people will be dependent on Medicaid to pay their bills. If Medicaid dries up, and only 10 percent of retirees have LTC insurance, private pay is the only option. On average, seven out of ten people will have used up their savings to pay for care. If there is no money and no Medicaid, it becomes a real crisis.

Retirees Two Major Worries

The two major things that retirees are worried about are running out of money and the high cost of health care. This is for good reason. One goes hand in hand with the other. The lack of preparation for the high cost of care is the number one reason people become impoverished in retirement.

The average base rate of an assisted-living community in Oregon is $3,628 per month. Home health care is $3,861 a month. The average cost for a private room in a nursing home is $8,943. A semiprivate room is $8,425 per month, which is $101,100 a year.

In order to private pay, seniors will have to come up with approximately $43,500 to $100,100 per year. Most people cannot pay out of pocket for more than eighteen months; therefore, there is a high risk of becoming impoverished.

To combat the pressure on Medicaid, the government has provided us with tax-free incentives to try to help us become financially independent so we can pay for our own care. I will discuss these options. One is the Pension Protection Act of 2006, which most people do not know is available. This is a very important option if we are to remain financially independent.

Most people do not know, that in some cases, they need to be in a facility such as a nursing home in order to receive Medicaid benefits. I don't know of anybody, including myself, who wants to go to a nursing home. If you want to learn how to stay in your own home for as long as possible and receive care benefits, you want to read this book.

Before we get into the heart of the book, I would like to tell you a little of my journey. I am including this so people know I am not just a financial specialist. I have lived through circumstances many others are going through. Because of my personal experience, I have been able to help many people with the process of a finding a facility for their loved one and gaining peace in having to place a family member in a facility (the hardest thing I have had to do in my life) while helping them protect their assets. Many of those I have helped relate my father's story to their family's story. Maybe you can also relate. Even though he passed some years ago, I still have to fight back the tears when I read about his life and what he meant to me as a father.

My Father before His Disease

Born and raised in West Monroe, Louisiana—where the *Duck Dynasty* family resides—my dad was a loving, giving father who made many sacrifices for us and others. He had an impeccable appearance, and he never had a hair out of place. He was a man's man but tenderhearted—and he had a line you didn't cross because he also had a fiery temper.

As a war veteran, he believed in honor and sacrifice, and he would fight for what he believed in. His brother said he was a fighter as a kid but after the war wanted nothing to do with it. If you hurt his family or challenged his honor, look out.

My memories were of him not as a fighter but as the person who took food to those who were hungry; drove the Sunday school bus after working long hours each week; taught us to drive, ride horses, and play ball; took us to martial arts classes; shared his time so we could go to gun-handling training to be safe hunters; and led our baseball team to the city championship. There were many more sacrifices he made. Was he tough? Yes. But he may have had the tenderest heart I have ever known.

He made no excuses about tearing up when he felt passionate about something. There is a picture of me at about age ten with tears in my eyes. My parents scheduled a professional photographer to take family pictures. When it was my time for a solo picture, the red in my eyes was very apparent. The reason for my tears was that Dad had gone hunting with my brother and had returned without a pheasant. While my brother was an excellent shot, my father couldn't hit anything. I don't remember him ever shooting a bird. I felt sorry for him.

As my brother and I got older, we would jab Dad about being such a terrible shot. Not until he passed did we find out the truth. We were stunned. Why do I think Dad chose not to shoot a bird? Because after reading his Separation Qualification Record from the army, under military qualification, it reads, "Sharpshooter Rifle Dec 45." Could he shoot? Apparently so! I believe he simply didn't want to kill anything like he didn't want to fight anymore. He had seen enough fighting and killing. My uncles told me my father had been through some horrific things in the war.

He Started to Change…His Strokes Turned into Dementia and the Hardest Day of My Life

After a series of undetectable strokes, which we found out about later from doctors, he started to change. No longer was he the father I knew and grew up with. He started to become a shell of what he had been. His children—who he sacrificed so much for—he didn't even know their names. His strokes had turned into dementia. At one point, he told his neighbor he didn't recognize my wife and me. He thought we were my mother's friends. He would repeat over and over, "I sure wish I could meet the boy who bought me these slippers."

I would say, "Dad, that was me."

He would say, "Oh," and then he would repeat the same thing over and over.

Like most adult children whose parent suffers from memory loss, it is normal to have a tormented heart. I know I did. One morning, I received a call no son wants to hear. My mother told me Dad was escorted home by the police after they found him wandering the streets. He was looking for his home—not the one he lived in for more than thirty years but the one in his mind. I knew what was coming next, and my stomach turned into knots.

My mother said, "I need you to come here and take your father to a care facility. I can't do this anymore."

The drive from Tigard, Oregon, to Richland, Washington, seemed like an eternity. I knew what awaited me was probably the most difficult thing I would ever face. Fear gripped me, and my heart was breaking. Fortunately, I have a strong, loving, and compassionate wife. Without her, I am not sure I would have made it through.

After we took him to the facility, he looked at me and said, "You know how to get me home, don't you?"

I collapsed emotionally. Walking out of what would be his new residence, I broke down. I felt I was abandoning him. I came to understand—and I have shared this with clients over the years who were facing the same challenge—our loved ones don't see where they have lived as home anymore. They are looking for someplace else, be it where they grew up or a picture they have seen and identify with. Even if Dad wanted me to take him home, I couldn't. I didn't know where his home was.

My father was always wound pretty tight. Not until he contracted dementia did he become more peaceful. He would pat my hand, along with other people he would come across, and say, "God bless you." He had a gentleness in his eyes. I would tell family and friends he had one foot in heaven and one on earth. There was a contentment he never had in his "normal" years. I felt more peaceful in his presence. If someone has to deal with memory loss, I hope and pray they get the kind my dad had.

My father-in-law said, "Growing older isn't for wimps."

I would add, "Dealing with a loved one who needs care isn't easy either."

The past eighteen years have been a journey that has given me purpose and meaning. After losing my father to Alzheimer's and being threatened with the devastating cost associated with his care, I set out to help other families who have disabled loved ones faced with the same concerns. I wasn't sure where the journey would take me, but I knew I wanted to help. This book will share what I have learned over the past eighteen years.

I Would Like to Help

Some years ago, in a room full of people, I got a tap on the shoulder. The gentleman who tapped me said, "David, good for you, and for what you do, but I don't see how there is any money in your specialty."

I had just given a presentation on asset protection to financial planners in the Northwest, and he was one of them. I responded, "Money isn't everything."

Life is also about passion, and I am passionate about the path I have taken. If I can help a person who saved all their working years protect their savings when faced with the high cost of care, I can feel good about that. We all make our choices.

I would also like to assist you in your journey and give you peace of mind by providing options to help safeguard your assets and your family. This book will give you information few know. It is my desire to serve your needs. Congratulations on purchasing this book. As Benjamin Franklin said, "An investment in knowledge pays the best interest."

May God bless you.

David Almond

CHAPTER 1

Caring for an aging parent

Placing a Loved One in a Care Facility

As I mentioned in the introduction, one of the hardest things in my life was taking my father to a care facility. Over the years, I have found it to be one of the most difficult challenges for clients I have worked with. We feel like we're taking them away from their homes and putting them in strange places.

I learned, and I've shared with many others, that our disabled loved ones suffering from advanced dementia don't recognize home any longer. In my father's case, he was wandering the streets and looking for where he grew up. It really shook me when he said, "You know how to take me home, don't you?" After thinking about it, I realized he didn't know where home was. Therefore, I wouldn't know where to take him, because his home was not a reality.

Many people I have helped really struggle with this and fight taking their loved ones to facilities. The risk becomes the caregiver becoming ill because of the stress of taking care of their own life and the challenge of taking care of a disabled loved one.

It is amazing how fast people can adapt to their new homes at facilities. A client, could no longer take care of his wife, who had dementia. He took her to a memory-care facility, told her he needed to take a business trip, and explained that he was leaving her "with these nice people." She adapted very quickly.

When on the fence about placing a loved one in a care community, consider a few important points:

- You can visit your love one anytime and stay as long as you would like. You are not sending them off to never see them again. Moving them to a care setting allows you to go to your home and get some peace and rest.
- Most people have never experienced taking care of a disabled person. Community care givers do it for a living. They are professionally trained. Sure there are below average facilities but by thoroughly checking the place out (I suggest going in at night time when the administrator and top management is not there) you should be able to determine their quality of care.
- Many times Medicaid does not pay for home health care. The impaired person has to reside in a facility to receive benefits. If you are trying to protect your savings, placing your loved one in a facility to get

them Medicaid qualified can make sense. This can substantially cut your expenses and help protect your assets.

Placing a family member in a professional long-term care setting can be a challenge. A family needs to weigh the effect it has on all. It is one of the most difficult decisions anyone will every face. Keep in mind the decision can be reversed, it isn't carved in stone. I wish you the best in whatever you decide.

Choosing a Care Community

As I stated, one of the most difficult challenges is choosing a care facility. From my experience, it is beneficial to find a continual-care community. As people age, it becomes more challenging to move them as their needs increase. For example, a person who can no longer take care of his/her day-to-day necessities at their residence is better off in a setting where they have less stress and can get help if required. In today's world, families are dispersed around the country because of job opportunities and other reasons. It becomes difficult to be available when a parent has a need. An independent-living apartment is often easier on them when qualified people are around to help them if it is warranted.

In a continual-care community, there are different levels of help available, including independent living, assisted living, and skilled care. Some also have memory care. The advantage is the parent can be moved to different units as their needs warrant. They will not have to experience a move to a whole new environment with all new people.

An important note: If you plan on getting your parent Medicaid qualified, the facility you choose must be a licensed Medicaid facility.

What the Facility Might Tell You Regarding Pay

When I was searching for a facility for my dad, I was told by the admissions person we would have to private pay for a few years before we could go on Medicaid. I was told this by three different facilities. Working in this field for several years, I knew they were in violation of their Medicaid license. An elder-law attorney I work with told me her client was recently given the same information.

In some states, they can get away with it. In Washington State, a state-licensed facility can require private pay for a period of time before one can go on Medicaid. If the facility is federally licensed, they are in violation if they require private pay. In Oregon, plain and simple, they cannot require private pay for any time period. The majority of facilities are Medicaid licensed. Even though they get paid less from the state than they receive from those private paying, they do not want empty beds. It's better to get a reduced amount than to get nothing at all.

If a facility in Oregon says you have to private pay, ignore them. If you live in another state, check with an elder-law attorney. Also check with the Department of State's Office of the Ombudsman. They are a great resource.

CHAPTER 2

Who pays for care? Medicare, reverse mortgages, health insurance, and the ACA

Does Medicare Pay For Long-Term Care?

Many Americans believe that Medicare pays for long-term care. In *Age Power*, Dr. Dychtwald refers to a study conducted by the University of Pennsylvania School of Social Work. They surveyed a thousand adults and asked them a range of financial questions; 53 percent believed Medicare pays for nursing home care. Dr. Dychtwald states, "This misperception leads to confusion and frequently results in tragic outcomes."

Furthermore, there is a glaring misunderstanding of the difference between Medicare and Medicaid. Medicare covers medical needs if you are sixty-five or older—regardless of your financial condition. Medicaid is a program based on financial need that pays benefits only to those who qualify.

Boiled down to its bare bones, Medicare pays for skilled care up to one hundred days. Medicare pays 100 percent of care for the first twenty days. Days 21 through 100 require a copay; Medicare pays a portion, and you pay a portion. In order for Medicare to pay, you have to receive your care from a Medicare-certified facility. In addition, a three-day hospital stay is required. Medicare pays only for skilled care—not custodial care. Custodial care activities are those needed to function on a day-to-day basis. Called activities of daily living (ADLs), these include such things as eating, transferring, bathing, dressing, toileting, and continence. Medicare's limitations create two problems:

> Many of our elders need custodial care due to aging and cognitive impairment such as Alzheimer's. Since these conditions don't require a three-day hospital stay, Medicare doesn't help.

> Since ADLs don't require a skilled nurse, a doctor, or a trained physical therapist, once again, Medicare isn't the answer.

Generally speaking, if it can't be cured or fixed outright, Medicare isn't going to pay for your health care requirements past one hundred days. Now you know what the majority of the population does not know: Medicare is not the solution for our long-term-care needs. Although this topic will not make you the center of attention at parties, knowing what you now know will help you better prepare for the future.

Reverse Mortgages

We hear a lot about reverse mortgages and their benefits. It seems like every time I turn on the television, Tom Selleck is promoting them. For those who need additional money to pay bills or pay for health care services, this can be a viable option. In the past few years, reverse mortgages have become very popular.

A reverse mortgage is a loan for seniors age sixty-two and older. They are insured by the Federal Housing Administration (FHA) and allow homeowners to convert some of their home equity into cash. As long as they're living in the home, they do not have to pay this back. The borrower must pay property taxes and insurance and keep up with the FHA guidelines. They can receive a lump sum or line of credit.

A reverse mortgage can work well to pay for long-term care if one can stay in the home. As people age and their physical limitations become greater, it can be difficult for them to continue to live there. If they have to move to assisted living, foster care, or a nursing home, the cost of the reverse mortgage comes due and is payable at that time. Therefore, they might be in a position of having to sell the home. For people who want to pass their home to their heirs, this can be an issue. If medically healthy enough, they may be able to qualify for life insurance, giving them the option of paying off the mortgage and allowing them to pass the house to the heirs.

Moving from the home creates another issue. The residence is exempt for Medicaid purposes if the Medicaid applicant continues to live in the home. If they move out, they lose the exemption. In this situation, planning needs take place, and a strategy must be used to help protect assets.

Does Health Insurance Pay for Care?

Many people believe that their medical insurance will pay long-term-care costs. In general, health insurance policies cover only very limited and specific types of long-term care. Like Medicare, it generally covers only skilled care for a short period of time, which is different from long-term care.

While health insurance is necessary for doctor visits, hospitalization, and other health issues, it is not designed to pay for custodial care when suffering from cognitive impairment or needing help with ADLs. The only insurance that does that is traditional long-term-care insurance, asset-based insurance, and annuity long-term-care insurance. Health insurance policies, as well as disability policies, are not the answer to our long-term-care needs.

Affordable Care Act

The Nationwide Financial Retirement Institute conducted a survey and found that seven in ten baby boomers think that the Affordable Care Act covers long-term care. The Affordable Care Act originally contained a provision called the Class Act, which created a public long-term-care insurance arrangement. Opponents of the provision repealed it due to cost. The Obama administration admitted the program couldn't be sustained. That being the case, we cannot look to the ACA to help us pay for care.

If Medicare, reverse mortgages (if you have to move to a facility), health insurance, and the ACA do not pay for long-term care, the options are self-pay, insurance, or Medicaid. Knowing this, you are now in a better position to protect your assets.

CHAPTER 3

Annuities...Providing income security and asset protection

The main facts I would like you to gain from this chapter are twofold:

1. The only financial product after the Deficit Reduction Act (DRA) of 2005 available to qualify for Medicaid benefits is a Medicaid Compliant Annuity which I will cover.

2. The only financial product available to provide income you cannot outlive is a life payout annuity which I will also include in this chapter.

Unfortunately, this chapter can be a little dry, but I need to include the technical features of annuities. Certain ones play a key role in asset protection, including, fixed, index, single premium, and annuities with life payouts. In the Preplanning chapter, I cover protection using fixed and index annuities, so having a basic understanding of how they function is important.

As you may be aware, there is a lot of negative press regarding annuities. In my book *The Seven Steps to a Worry-Free Retirement,* I address these objections and how annuities are misunderstood. Those who make these negative statements are not experts in asset protection and how annuities are the only game in town to qualify for Medicaid and the only resource for income you can't outlive.

As we deal with living longer and making smart money choices, studies conducted by the National Bureau of Economic Research and the Brookings Institute along with MIT, Yale, Harvard, and others have concluded that a life annuity adds more security to retirees. Therefore, more people are putting income security in their portfolio by using annuities that pay out for life.

So grab some coffee and hang with me.

Annuity Basics and How They Are Taxed

An annuity is a written contract between an insurance company, an owner, and an annuitant. Many times, the owner and annuitant are the same person. The contract is unilateral, meaning that the insurance company cannot break the contract, but the owner can. Under the agreement, the owner and not the annuitant, if different people, has all rights. As shown in figure 1, while money is in the annuity, under Internal Revenue Code (IRC) section 72(c), it is not taxable. In other words, it is tax deferred, which is similar to money in a retirement account.

The concept is simple: If we can get a loan from the government by deferring taxes, we can use the government's money to compound in our own account. Money that was leaking through our fingertips is now captured and used for our benefit. One reason pension plans, IRAs, and annuities are so popular is because they function pretty much the same way.

When putting money in the annuity, you have the option of choosing between a onetime lump sum or a flexible premium annuity that allows ongoing contributions. When taking money out, the owner has the option of taking it one of two ways: random withdrawals or tax-favored income. Another term for tax-favored income is annuitization. When one annuitizes the contract, he or she is exchanging the money in the annuity for a stream of income. This is key to understanding how a Medicaid Compliant Annuity functions.

While you can reach in and take money out of an annuity at any time, a penalty may be assessed if you do so during the surrender-charge period. Most companies provide a liquidity feature and allow you to take 10 percent of the total amount in the annuity as a withdrawal during a contract year without penalty. To give an additional layer of security, some companies provide a feature called principal guarantee. Principal guarantee means that you will never get back less than what you put into the annuity minus withdrawals. For example, if you decided to take out all of your money during the surrender-charge period, the penalty cannot dip into your principal. The worst-case scenario is that you may lose the accrued interest.

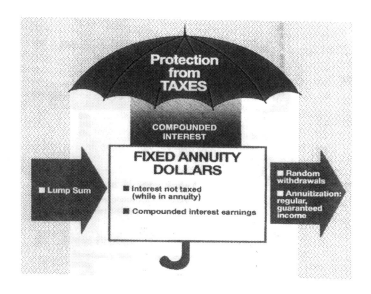

Figure 1

Originally designed to provide retirement income, most people use annuities for the tax-deferral benefit. Retirees have caught on to this opportunity, and many use annuities to cut taxes. Rarely in the past have annuity owners taken money out. 73 percent plan on only tapping their annuity for catastrophic illness or to pay nursing home costs (2013 Gallup)

Most pass away without ever touching the money. In the Preplanning chapter, I will show you how to leverage and get tax-free money from the government while protecting yourself against the high cost of care.

As I mentioned, annuities benefit from tax-deferred compounding like retirement plans such as a 401(k), 403(b), IRA, and so on. Graph 2 shows the power of tax deferral. In this example, a person in a 24 percent tax bracket sets aside $100,000 for fifteen years and receives a 7 percent return. You can see the difference if one pays taxes on the interest every year compared to using the government's money to help build a bigger pot of capital. I don't know about you, but when it comes to financial security, I'll take the bigger pot of money.

Benefit from Tax Deferred Growth

- Tax-deferred compounding
- Over time, more actual dollars

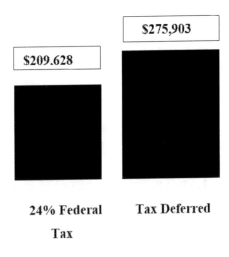

Graph 2

LET'S TAKE LOOK AT THE VARIOUS TYPES OF ANNUITIES.

Fixed Annuity

With a fixed annuity, an insurance company pays a fixed rate of return for a specified period of time. The rate can be fixed for the term of the annuity, or it can change each contract year. If you are curious about when the contract year started, you can check the policy or call the agent or company. Fixed annuities are the choice of most retirees since they are similar to certificates of deposit (CD). Like a CD, an annuity pays a fixed interest rate for a period of time, and penalties are assessed if taken out early.

A CD is issued by the bank, and therefore FDIC insured—if too much money is not put in the CD—but the annuity is issued by an insurance company. While insurance companies have safety nets to help protect the public against insolvency, such as legal reserves and the State Guarantee Association, it is still important to find out the financial ratings of the insurance company.

Index Annuity

You've probably seen commercials talking about index annuities. There is one on TV a lot that talks about an investment that only goes forward and never back, up and never down, and you cannot lose money even if the stock market is down. Although the gentleman in the commercial does not mention index annuities outright, that's what he's talking about.

A feather in the cap for index annuities is that they have recently outperformed bonds. Their returns have been better. I find they're very popular in the senior market. Investors tend to get better returns than in bank products or fixed annuities.

While fixed and variable annuities were popularized in the 1970s, index annuities came on the scene in 1995. Index annuities are kind of a hybrid of fixed and variable annuities. Index annuities share some of the same features. The fixed annuity provides a specified rate of return, the variable annuity allows for a return with no ceiling and no safety net should the market drop, and the index annuity meets somewhere in the middle. The index annuity earns a minimum rate of interest and offers the potential for excess interest based on the performance of an index such as the S&P 500. Unlike the variable annuity, whereby you can lose money if the market goes down, the index annuity is protected from market risk. An owner does not share in the market loss or receive all of the market gain.

With an index annuity, the owner will participate in the gain up to a cap or participation rate. The caps and participation rates can vary from annuity to annuity and company to company. Based on a participation formula, the owner receives interest credited to their account annually. Once the interest is credited to the owner, it can never be lost—even if the market subsequently declines. How the interest is credited also varies from company to company.

In *Index Annuities: Power and Protection*, Jack Marrion, a recognized expert, states,

I've done enough analysis to see that all of these other crediting methods should produce about the same results if you wait long enough—unless you know for certain how the stock market will move in the future—so the key is picking an index annuity carrier that will treat you well down the road.

Those who purchase index annuities typically do not have the temperament for the stock market, but they want the opportunity for a greater return than a bank product or fixed annuity can give them. For those who want a guarantee and are satisfied with less than the overall market return—in my opinion—an index annuity is a good option.

Single Premium Immediate Annuity

A single premium immediate annuity is simply putting money in an annuity and immediately receiving income. Unlike annuities that grow tax deferred, the immediate annuity skips the deferral stage and goes directly into the payout stage. If you have received a pension from a company, it works much the same. All annuities have an income feature that allows either what is called a systematic withdrawal or annuitization. The difference is with most companies, you can take a systematic withdrawal either occasionally or continually, whatever your particular need is at the time. Keep in mind if you are still in the surrender-charge period, if you take in excess of what the company allows—which is usually 10 percent—you may be subject to a penalty. If you choose to annuitize, some of the old-style policies will not allow you to change your decision once you make it.

When an owner annuitizes the contract, he or she is exchanging the money in the annuity for a stream of income. Choices include lifetime income that cannot be outlived or a specified period of time with many options in between. While annuitization has been rarely used, it is becoming more prominent to help eliminate income risk. Most retirees have greater peace of mind receiving a guaranteed income and not having to worry about market fluctuations.

Taxation of Annuities

While annuities grow tax deferred during the accumulation stage, they are taxed when money comes out. If you reach in and take money out, you are taxed on the interest first. For example, you put $50,000 into an annuity, it has grown to $60,000, and you want to take a withdrawal. The first $10,000—the deferred gain—is taxed as ordinary income. If you dip into the $50,000, it is not taxed since it is considered a return of principal.

In the case of annuitization, taxation is treated differently. In the example above, once a payout period is chosen, let's say five years, the $60,000 would be paid out plus interest over the time period. The IRS considers the payment interest plus a return of principal, and they allow an exclusion ratio similar to selling real estate on a contract. Each payment received consists of part principal and part interest. If the overall return paid is $60,000, and the initial investment is $50,000, the formula is $50,000 divided by

$60,000 or 83 percent (rounded for simplicity). For every payment received, 83 percent of it is not taxable. Why is this important? It provides us an opportunity to receive income, tax efficiently.

Annuities... Protecting Assets from the Cost of Long-Term Care

Annuities issued by insurance companies (as opposed to private annuities) are an important financial product that can protect the assets of a husband and wife when one of them needs long-term care. Also, it is the only financial product that the government accepts as a vehicle to guard against having to spend down assets in order to qualify for Medicaid. If used correctly, an annuity will help protect a married couple and a single disabled person from becoming impoverished. It can be the bridge between financial security and asset depletion. However, if used incorrectly for Medicaid-planning purposes, it can do more damage than good.

Several years ago, I received a phone call from an elder-law attorney regarding a rejected Medicaid application. He had gotten my name from another attorney I had worked with for several years, and I had done her client's Medicaid annuities. She told him to call me to see if I could remedy the situation.

The attorney's client applied for Medicaid benefits and was turned down because the annuity they submitted, which they thought met the rules, did not. Apparently, the insurance agent took the client's deferred annuity and annuitized it—but did so past the client's life expectancy.

In order for the annuity to comply with Medicaid rules, it has to be "actuarially sound"—and this annuity wasn't. It created chaos.

The attorney asked if I could fix it. I told him I didn't think the insurance company would want the liability, so I contacted the company and was able to get it reversed. We corrected the annuity application, and a Medicaid-compliant annuity was issued. We reapplied to the state and sent in the annuity, and it was approved. The attorney and I became very good friends and did a lot of fly-fishing and business together.

In this chapter, I lay out the rules an annuity must meet in order for it to be compliant in the state of Oregon. The rules can vary slightly between states, but the Medicaid annuity is generally accepted.

I get upset when people with limited incomes and savings get bad advice from trusted resources. The thing that is so sad about this predicament is many people run out of money when they do not have to. Being faced with life-altering care needs is stressful enough without worrying about going broke.

Medicaid Compliant Annuities

Some professionals thought that Medicaid annuities, as an asset-protection strategy, would be wiped out by the government with the creation of the Deficit Reduction Act of 2005 (DRA 2005). I thought so too. I am glad I was wrong. While the government did put some restrictions on the use of annuities, they are alive and well when using them for the protection of the healthy spouse.

The use of annuities will be key for many facing long-term care who do not have—and cannot qualify for—long-term-care insurance. For those of you who have loved ones faced with long-term care and are worried about being able to pay the bills, this section is critical.

The Deficit Reduction Act (DRA) of 2005 eliminated most asset-protection strategies except for the Medicaid Compliant Annuity (MCA). The MCA is commonly used by many elder-law attorneys and long-term-care specialists, like myself, to help people keep the savings they have even if they're currently in a long-term-care facility.

People own more than $2 trillion in deferred annuities, and the majority are owned by seniors. Working with seniors over the years, I have found many believe a deferred annuity will protect them from the high costs of long-term care. In most cases, that simply is not true. They were told that by the person selling them the annuity. In most states, including Oregon, they have to be Medicaid compliant. What does that mean?

They must be:

- irrevocable,
- nontransferable,
- no cash value,
- level payments, and
- actuarially sound.

Irrevocable

Irrevocable typically applies when a consumer is exchanging a lump sum of money for a stream of payments from an insurance company or when a tax-deferred annuity is converted to a payout mode. Once the insurance company determines how much the payments will be to the customer and the number of payments (term of the contract) has been agreed upon, it cannot be changed. In other words, the annuity owner and insurance company are obligated to stay with the agreed-upon structure. In addition to not being able to change the payment amount or period certain/term, the contract must be irrevocable as to its parties, beneficiaries, and so forth. The contract cannot allow the owner to change anything about the contract after it's purchased. The contract is then irrevocable.

Nontransferable

We have all seen the commercial where the people are yelling out the window, "It is my money, and I want it now." Their desire is to turn their payments into a lump sum. Companies such as J. G. Wentworth and Peachtree are happy to buy the income stream for discounted cash. J. G. or Peachtree receive the payments, and the annuity owner receives cash.

If you can sell the annuity on the secondary market to companies such as J. G. Wentworth and Peachtree, your annuity it is not exempt; therefore, you would have to spend it to get Medicaid qualified, which could create disqualification for months if not years. An MCA can get a married couple qualified quickly and a single person an opportunity to save a lot of their assets and still receive Medicaid benefits. Most annuities that people own are not MCAs. A non-MCA can be exchanged tax-free for an MCA. Only a handful of companies offer MCAs.

No Cash Value

There cannot be any cash left in the annuity after the payout period.

Level Payments

All payments from the annuity have to be level, meaning they have to be the same amount for every payment.

Actuarially Sound

This varies from state to state. Oregon requires the payout to be made within twelve months of the Medicaid applicant's life expectancy. It cannot be past their life expectancy.

What if you have an annuity that does not meet the Medicaid-compliant rules? If you own a nonqualified (non-IRA) annuity, you can exchange it tax-free by way of a 1035 exchange. Only a handful of insurance companies issue Medicaid annuities. Make sure you work with someone who is qualified to do an exchange that meets the tax as well as the Medicaid rules. If your annuity is in the surrender-charge period, you may be charged to exchange it.

This leads me to how you can receive tax deferral with a competitive rate of return. No 1035 exchange is required, and surrender charges do not apply.

Pre-Planning Using a Taxed Deferred Annuity

Many deferred annuities are owned by a husband and wife. If one spouse becomes disabled, it's important to use the Medicaid-Compliant Annuity (MCA) to protect assets.

The challenge is that some insurance companies make it a taxable event to change ownership into one spouse's name. That can be very costly. The deferred gains will be taxable. If you are under fifty-nine and a half, you may also pay a 10 percent penalty. If you take money out while the annuity is in the surrender-charge period, the surrender charge can be expensive.

So what's the answer? The answer is to use an insurance company that will provide the same benefits: tax deferral and a competitive rate of return like you would get from another company. The difference is this company will allow ownership to be transferred into one spouse's name when it's owned by both spouses without taxation. Also, that annuity can become a MCA, which other insurance companies typically don't do. How does that work? Let's say you have an annuity that you purchased three years ago. It is still in surrender charge, meaning you would pay a percentage of the annuity if you moved it or surrendered it. As I mentioned earlier, people can move from a non-MCA, without taxation, to an MCA. This is what's called a 1035 exchange for nonqualified money. If it is qualified money, such as an IRA, 401(k), 403(b), you can do a nontaxable exchange using a trustee-to-trustee transfer.

If the annuity is still in surrender, surrender charges would apply. It can be expensive to transfer to an MCA; even if surrender charges apply, they are relatively less expensive than private paying for care. There is a company, The Standard in Portland Oregon, that provides tax-deferred growth and a competitive interest rate, as would another company, but the difference is even if the annuity is still in surrender The Standard will waive the surrender charges and turn it into a MCA without taxation. There is no need for a 1035 exchange or a trustee-to-trustee transfer. It is all done internally.

If you would like to position your savings and investments to help protect them, you might consider this strategy. One caveat: Medicaid rules could change in the future, making this option void. Keep in mind you would still have a tax-deferred annuity. If the option is still available at the time you need it, you are probably better off.

Protection Against Outliving Your Income

Various studies are emerging that promote the use of annuities to guard against *longevity risk*. Why is that? In the past, retirees received two sources of guaranteed income: Social Security and company pension plans or defined-benefit plans (DB). According to a 2015 Bureau of Labor Statistics study, only 13 percent of nonunion retirees received income from DB plans. Employers have found it too expensive to fund them. The shift by companies away from defined-benefit plans is continuing to increase. Employers have switched from providing income to retirees to putting the burden on those in retirement to make their own money last a lifetime. The exiting employee walks away with their qualified plan, 401(k), 403(b), and so on, and is now faced with making their money last for a lifetime.

What does the reduction in DB plans and Social Security benefits mean to retirees? Less guaranteed income to pay for needs. We can no longer say, "I was loyal to the company, and now they will take care of me." It is up to us to make our own money last, and the stakes are high. If we are not successful, we can no longer look to the company that employed us. Instead, we must look to ourselves.

Many financial professionals believe that those who want to maintain their standard of living in retirement will need to replace 70–80 percent of the income they made during their working years. From my experience, I think 70–80 percent is low, and here is why. Due to modern technology, medical breakthroughs, and healthier lifestyles, we tend to be more active at retirement age than our parents were. During the first several years, many travel and are on the go. Because of increased activity, dialing down spending does not usually happen. As we age, most of us slow down a little more, which starts to curtail spending. That being said, I believe many retirees will be in for a rude financial awakening if they underestimate their spending needs in retirement, especially since 78 percent of retirees do not have a financial plan.

So what we have is the demise of guaranteed income from companies in the form of DB plans, greater activity in retirement leading to more spending, and we are living longer (longevity risk). A smaller population of workers will be asked to provide Social Security income benefits for the largest number of people entering retirement in history. Social Security benefits are dropping, and the system is currently unfunded, which should tell us that depending on Social Security for a portion of our retirement income is shaky at best.

What is the answer? We need our own defined benefit plan—a plan we cannot outlive—a guaranteed flow of lifetime income. How do we do it? By using a life annuity. A life annuity can provide more income for a longer period of time than other savings or investment options. In addition, a life-income annuity provides a higher rate of return than one can get on a similar, but unannuitized portfolio. Annuitants (those receiving the income) benefit from *mortality premium*, which equates to an additional rate of return. By design, an annuity can provide us with our own inexhaustible pension for as many years as we are on this earth. The end result is more security that we cannot outlive.

Many financial experts have come to the conclusion that a life annuity adds the greatest security to retirees; some of the most prominent in the world are Nobel Prize winners. Studies supporting this conclusion have been conducted at MIT, Wharton, Berkley, Yale, Harvard, London Business School, Hebrew University, Carnegie Mellon, and others.

Here is another supporting study:

A study from National Bureau of Economic Research and The Brookings Institution

Retirees increasingly are self-insuring against a variety of retirement risks, especially the risk of outliving their assets. One alternative to self-insuring against extended longevity is an insurance product known as a *longevity annuity*. This type of annuity pays income for as long as the insured lives.

Longevity annuities remain a product that relatively few consumers know about. The experiment showed that, among a group subject to a lump-sum distribution in a laboratory setting, 60 percent elected to purchase a longevity annuity when presented with the option to do so (Gazzale and Walker 2009).

> *We are optimistic that longevity annuities can significantly increase expected lifetime well-being for middle- and upper-income retirees who have substantial financial assets at the time of retirement. Studies show retirees have more peace of mind when they have guaranteed income and don't have to worry about market volatility.*

Although it may be tempting, I caution you not to go out and buy a life annuity. If you do it wrong, you may not be able to fix it. An incorrect purchase of a life annuity can chip away at your standard of living in later years. Do some planning and make sure that what you are doing—or plan on doing—is right for you.

As a Certified Financial Planner, I've helped my clients add security income to their retirement through the defined-benefit concept. I've also added another element of security by positioning the DB plan to be converted for the purpose of Medicaid eligibility in case long-term care is needed down the road.

The following case study follows the theme of this book, which is addressing the two main fears of seniors facing: running out of money and the high cost of health care. This case study also adds a third element: additional protection for the heirs.

Case Study: Helen (not her real name)

An attorney sent me Helen's situation. She had an income shortfall:

- 84 years old
- $184,000 in savings
- needs more income
- she is healthy but concerned about LTC if needed in the future
- does not want to do a Medicaid annuity
- family concerns about a quote they received for a life-only annuity payout (no benefits to the heirs)

Helen, like so many seniors, did not own LTC insurance.

Helen's son and daughter had an insurance agent run a proposal using an annuity to pay out through her life expectancy. It was a life-only option. The daughter was concerned that if Mom should die prematurely, the insurance company would get the remainder of money, which is correct. A life-only option was not the answer for this family. With a life-only payout, there would be no money left for the heirs. The attorney was concerned about Helen needing Medicaid in the future. The attorney asked me to run an illustration based on Helen's life expectancy, which was seven and a half years. The annuity would be Medicaid compliant under the Oregon rules.

Helen felt she was healthy and was concerned that her money would be gone if we did a seven-year payout and she lived past seven and a half years, and she was correct. What if, after seven years, she did not need LTC and was broke? The attorney told me that her son, who was power of attorney, wanted to talk with me about the annuity option and how it would work in this situation. He was an airline pilot and a very sharp individual.

We talked for some time, and I explained the process.

He said, "Dave, Mom will not go for a seven-year payout … period."

I told him to let me think about the answer.

My Challenge

- Helen wanted income to cover her shortfall along with income security for life (a DB) plan.
- The heirs wanted to make sure they were not disinherited should Helen die prematurely.
- The attorney wanted Medicaid planning (asset protection) should Helen need long-term care in the future

What I came up with pleased the attorney and the family. The answer was an annuity with a life payout and a seven-year period certain. Helen will have income for the rest of her life. If she lives past seven and a half years, she's won the lottery. The insurance company has to pay her for as long as she lives. The policy guarantees the family will receive an inheritance should she pass before seven years.

The heirs were happy with the solution, and Helen was too, but there was one problem. What if she needed long-term care in the future? The life annuity does not qualify as an MCA under the Oregon rules. I explained that we would simply convert the annuity to cash. At that time, she would gift the balance to family, creating a relatively short period of disqualification. After that ran out, she would qualify for Medicaid and still have assets left over for her quality of life. The solution turned out to be a win-win-win for Helen, the heirs, and the attorney.

While most financial planners look at meeting the income goals while investing for the future, due to my experience and background in asset protection, I always look at meeting the client's current needs while taking into account long-term-care strategies if the client should become disabled in the future.

CHAPTER 4

Crisis planning- Medicaid for those currently in care

I was recently talking with a colleague, and I mentioned that I have been drawn to Medicaid planning. I told him taxes bore me, and Medicare really bores me, but for whatever reason, Medicaid planning does not. Although it has government rules and can be highly technical, I enjoy the process. Recently an elder-law attorney I work with said that I was a geek like her. She's one of the most esteemed attorneys in the area, so I took that as a compliment.

I think I'm drawn to it because it is tangible. Helping retirees protect their hard-earned savings gives me great satisfaction.

What I am about to share with you few people know. If I asked one hundred retirees, maybe two would know how to protect assets when a loved one is in care paying those high monthly costs. The goal of this chapter is to equip you with the information you need to understand to keep you from being impoverished should the need for care arise or if you currently have a loved one in a facility.

The following is the nuts and bolts of asset-protection planning. It is the only way to protect savings when someone who is in a crisis and currently residing in a facility is rifling through their savings.

What is Medicaid?

Medicaid is a joint federal-state program created to help people with limited income and resources gain better access to health care. It operates within a federal framework, but it is implemented through state laws and administrative rules. There are nonfinancial eligibility requirements such as age, disability, and residency, as well as strict financial eligibility requirements. When one qualifies, the government will pay a portion of the long-term-care costs for the qualified individual.

Be advised that the rules for Medicaid vary from state to state. Problems arise when the states have varying interpretations or are slow to comply with the federal rules. I recommend that you work with a competent financial adviser/Medicaid-planning specialist and elder-law attorney who are familiar with the rules in your state before employing any Medicaid-planning strategies.

Because this section is not a complete study on Medicaid planning, I'll focus on hitting the high points and practical applications that you can use. I will also point out some of the traps and misunderstandings. As much as I have tried to steer away from it, in order to describe Medicaid-planning strategies used to protect assets, I must be somewhat technical in my explanations. If you think Medicaid planning may be applicable to your situation, the next step is seeking professional counsel.

LET'S FIRST AT THE TWO MEDICAID QUALIFICATION RULES

INCOME TEST

In 2018, in Oregon, a Medicaid applicant can be receiving $2,250 a month in income. The "name-on-the-check" rule is applied; if the applicant is receiving checks such as Social Security, pension, annuity, or any money being paid to them in their name, it falls under the income test. For the purposes of Medicaid eligibility, if an applicant's monthly income does not total more than $2,250, the income test is met. It is important to note that when applying, the spouse's income is considered separate.

What if his income is over $2,250 a month? Would that in and of itself disqualify a person for Medicaid services? Not in Oregon. Oregon is an "income-cap state," meaning that an *income cap trust* (also known as a "Miller Trust") could be drafted by a qualified attorney, which would allow income eligibility under the rules.

Note: Not all states are income-cap states. Most states are "spend-down" states, meaning that if a person spends his or her income (less the personal needs allowance) on care costs, he or she would still be eligible to receive Medicaid benefits for the balance of the costs if the other requirements are met.

THE ASSET TEST

For the purpose of Medicaid qualification, your home, car, and personal belongings are exempt and not considered resource assets. You are allowed to keep the following:

- principal residence (unless the single impaired person will not return to the home)
- one vehicle
- personal effects, furnishings, and jewelry (some states limit the value of these items)
- a burial plan or an irrevocable prepaid plan
- funeral or burial merchandise (casket, urn, cemetery plot, or vault)
- medical equipment, such as a wheelchair, may be allowed in some states
- a nominal amount of life insurance policies (typically $1,500)

A home, car, and personal belongings are protected and are not subject to "spend down." In other words, applicants are not required to spend or sell these resources in order to qualify for assistance. These are called "non-resource" assets.

In 2018, the community (healthy spouse) can keep half the assets up to $123,600. I will cover how a married couple can protect assets over the $123,600.

Note: Even if a husband and wife have separate investments and bank accounts, the state considers the money as if it is owned jointly. If the husband applies for Medicaid, even if his assets are separate, the state adds all the assets of both spouses together as if they are one.

Should you divorce to protect assets

I believe it is important to address divorce. Let me start out by saying, I think this is utterly ridiculous. The subject comes up, and I know of attorneys who have promoted it. Why in the world would a married couple get a divorce when somebody who has expertise and experience in Medicaid planning can protect their assets. I have come to the conclusion that those who promote divorce don't understand the rules and how to protect their client's savings.

Many people believe they married for life. A loving spouse would be there to support their disabled wife or husband. I'm not saying that wouldn't be the case if they got a divorce, but it would seem to have a cloud over it. I'm not the moral compass for anybody, but it appears logical to stay married when a couple can protect their life savings—even if one is in an LTC facility.

I will get into Medicaid planning for a couple and how their assets can be protected. I need to remind the reader that rules can change according to the federal government and the state you live in.

Medicaid Planning for Singles

The two application process

The Deficit Reduction Act (DRA) of 2005 was put in place to tighten Medicaid rules. The government does not want people to give their assets away and then apply for Medicaid and qualify. One of the areas they made more restrictive is the gifting of assets by a parent to their children and then being able to receive benefits.

In Oregon, a mother gives $84,250 to her children and then submits an application to the state to become Medicaid qualified. The state uses what's called the *divestment divisor* to determine the period of ineligibility. In this case, they would take $84,250 and divide it by the 2018 divisor of $8,425. The result would be ten months of ineligibility, meaning the mother cannot receive Medicaid benefits for ten months. It is important to note that she has to qualify for Medicaid other than the gift. What does this mean? It means that she cannot have more than $2,000 in her name, and she has to meet the nonfinancial qualifications such as the service standard requirement. Typically, the service standard requires that she needs help with things such as transferring, dressing, bathing, eating, continence, walking, or the activities of daily living (ADLs). Also, if she has cognitive impairment where she cannot be on her own and needs someone to cue her and help her with her day-to-day functioning, she would qualify. If she is independent and doesn't need help with her care, she would *not* qualify under the service requirement.

So let's say she qualifies other than the transfer of the $84,250. She isn't eligible for ten months and has to self-pay for that period of time. In some states the disabled person does not have to be a nursing home. It can be assisted living, adult foster care, a continual-care community, or a memory-care facility. In order to receive Medicaid benefits, she has to reside in a Medicaid-licensed facility.

How does the two application process work? I have done this several times for clients, and it has never failed.

In the above case, I make application to the state knowing there will be a ten-month period of ineligibility. If I am, as I am in most cases, the *authorized representative,* meaning I fill out the application, send it in, and communicate with the state on the client's behalf so the client does not have to be involved in the application process. Many times, people feel intimidated when answering questions from a state case worker. I take that stress away by acting on their behalf.

As the authorized representative, I would receive a form from the caseworker stating there is a period of eligibility. As mentioned, I knew that would happen, and it would be for ten months, which the document confirms. After the ten months is up, I reapply—and the client is approved.

Here is the secret to this process. Let's say the client is paying $7,500, a month which is typical for someone in memory care. She has Social Security and pension income equaling $2,000. That leaves her with a deficit of $5,500, ($7,500–$2,000). She has to pay $5,500 for ten months, which is $55,000. Remember how I had her transfer $84,250 to family while she paid $55,000 for care? That means the family is able to keep $29,250, which is a far cry from spending down to $2,000 and then applying.

Why am I doing this? My goal is not so much to provide an inheritance for the children even though that is very important to most seniors, especially women. The main reason for this process is for the mom's quality of life. Medicaid pays for room and board but no extras. If the family wants to take her on a trip, buy her new clothes, bedding, or whatever, they now have extra money to do that. So we're able to enhance the mom's quality of life while she is still with us. An interesting study was done years ago, and its findings were that when seniors, especially women, run out of money, they tend to pass away—so this process seems to have important results.

The moral of the story is this: Don't let anybody tell you it is a requirement to spend down to $2,000 to qualify for Medicaid.

Protecting mom from family financial mismanagement, divorce or lawsuit during the DQ period.

If we gift money to family members, what happens if they mismanage the money, go through a divorce, or are sued? That is a question that needs to be addressed.

In the example, the mom has gifted her assets, creating a ten months of ineligibility, and only has $2,000 in her name with a $7,500 bill each month. She is dependent on her family to pay for her care through the disqualification period. If nobody pays, she runs the risk of being asked to leave the facility.

Something else important needs to be addressed regarding gifting money to the family. Let's say there are three siblings: two brothers and a sister. They each received equal gifts. What happens if one of them passes away unexpectedly or has their assets frozen due to a divorce or lawsuit? Logically, it would fall on the other two siblings to pay the mom's bill. That being the case, the gifting amount would not be equitable and would put more responsibility on the other two siblings.

In the case where one passed away, their assets would probably flow via their Will or a Trust to their heirs. If the children of the deceased receive the money, they may choose not to pay for Grandma's care, leaving the responsibility on the shoulders of the other two siblings. What can be done to help protect the mom's money?

What I recommend provides the most security to the mom and the family. A single-premium immediate annuity provides more security. The annuity is a contract with the insurance company that obligates the company to make payments of a certain amount for a specified period of time. It is important that the company is financially very strong and has been in business for many years through good and bad financial times. The youngest company I work with is ninety years old, the others are more than one hundred years old. They have remained financially strong and highly rated even through the Depression and other difficult times.

We place the amount of money needed to pay for care through the ineligibility period in a Medicaid Compliant Annuity. The insurance company sends the payment to the mom's checking account, which can be the same account she uses for her pension and Social Security. The power of attorney or the individual who writes the payment to the facility would continue to do so. The annuity strategy eliminates the possibility of a family member mismanaging the money, passing away prematurely, going through a divorce, or getting sued. This approach takes the money management away from the mom's children and makes it an obligation of the insurance company. This provides much more security and ensures that the mom's money is there to pay her bill through the ineligibility period.

Once I explain the benefits of the annuity to the family, they like it because it takes the obligation off of them and the fear of something going wrong and jeopardizing the mom's security. For anyone looking to protect a loved one in care, this strategy adds peace of mind for those involved.

Immediate Medicaid qualification…turning a spend-down asset into an income stream.

In evaluating Medicaid financial qualification, the state looks at two areas: assets and income. If an individual applies for benefits and has $50,000 in savings, when they can only have $2,000, the state will say, "You have to spend down the remaining $48,000 and then come back and apply." The secret to qualification under the rules is turning the asset into income. By doing so, it is no longer subject to spend down since it is now income.

An example of this is the client with $50,000, instructed to spend down $48,000, can become immediately qualified for Medicaid using this income strategy (assuming they have met the service requirements).

Elder law attorneys and long-term care/Medicaid specialists, like me, will put the $48,000 in a Medicaid-compliant annuity to turn an asset into income. In Oregon the payments would be set up based on the client's life expectancy (in some states the payout can be shorter than life expectancy). Income is paid to the client monthly for a specified period of time. The downside is the income from the annuity would have to be paid toward the client's care. If the client is in a facility, the money would go to that facility. So what's the advantage of doing this if the money has to go to pay for care? Let's take a look how this can be advantageous for the client and the family.

Case Study

Case Specifics for Joan Smith

- Countable Assets- $440,000
- Cost of Care- $7,500 a Month
- Social Security- $1,500 a Month
- Shortfall - $6,000
- Age 80
- S.S Table Life Expectancy 9.73 years
- Due to health issues besides dementia not expected to live past two years

Objective: Get Joan Medicaid qualified as soon as possible to reduce costs, saving her and her family the difference between private pay and Medicaid reimbursement.

1. **Spend- Down Amount**- $440,000- $2,000 = $438,000

2. **Eliminate Spend-Down**- Purchase a Medicaid Compliant Annuity that meets Oregon rules of being within 12 months of life expectancy.

Annuity Invest.	Period Certain	Monthly Payout	Total Payout
$438,000	108 Months	$4112	$444,049

3. **Determine Monthly Savings** – Private Pay $7,500 – Medicaid Pay $5,551= **$1,949**

4. **Joan lives 24 months. Total Facility Payment Savings**- $1949 * 24 = **$ 46,776**

5. **Determine Balance Left to Heirs from Annuity**- Payment to the facility from the annuity is $98,688 ($4112 * 24 = $98,688). * No reimbursement to the state due to Joan's payment to the facility was

greater than the state reimbursement for Memory Care of $3,870.

6. **Total Savings From Immediate Medicaid Qualification**

- Balance to Heirs from Annuity $345,361
- + Total Facility Payment Savings   <u>$46,776</u>
- = Total Family Savings $392,137

7. **Determine Medicaid Planning Savings Over Private Pay**

- Private Pay Savings- $440,000- $144,000 (24 months @ $6,000 shortfall) = $296,000
- Annuity Savings - $444,049- $98,688 (paid from annuity) =$345,361
- Total Medicaid Planning Savings- $49,361 ($345,361-$296,000)

Not Planning- If Joan did not plan and continued to live, her $440,000 in savings would have been depleted in a little over 6 years. The money left in the annuity after 6 years for heirs would = **$148,032** (108 month contractual payments – 72 months of payments = 36 payments left at $4,112 per month). The savings from the difference between private pay and Medicaid pay would = **$140,328** over 6 years (monthly savings of $1,949 over 72 months). This assumes her cost of care does not increase.

Service Contracts

The majority of caregivers are family members. If you want to save your family money, you will want to know about service contracts. In the case where a daughter is taking care of Mom and every now and then Mom writes her a check, the family might end up paying more for care than they need to. Why? Because the state considers the money given to the daughter a gift. If Mom and the family decide to have Mom apply for Medicaid benefits, the state will figure a period of ineligibility based on the amount of money the daughter received. This will keep Mom from becoming Medicaid qualified for a period of time. If Mom has paid the daughter for some years, it could result in a substantial disqualification.

The answer is to draft a service contract. In this situation, the daughter would be paid by the mother contractually for services provided. This would be like having a caregiver charging Mom for the time and professionalism provided.

There are a few options: One is to find a service contract form on the internet, complete it, and sign it. The form has to comply with state rules. The better option is to go to an elder-law attorney to make sure the service agreement is drafted in a way that the state will accept it when Medicaid is applied for. If done incorrectly, it could be denied by the state.

How expensive is it not to have a service contract? Let's say Mom is in a facility and paying $7,000 a month. If she was on Medicaid, the only thing she would pay to the facility would be her Social Security and pension (if she has one). If her pension and Social Security total $1,500, if on Medicaid, that is the maximum amount that she would be paying to the facility. If she has a period of ineligibility because of not having a service contract, she will have to private pay through the disqualification period. The difference between the cost of Medicaid and private pay would be $5,500 a month. If she had an ineligibility period of four months, she would be paying an additional $22,000 that would not have to be paid if she had a qualified service contract.

Even if you need to pay some money to an elder-law attorney to make sure the service contract is correct, it can save you a lot. The service contract is very important and shouldn't be overlooked when a family member is caring for a disabled loved one.

Medicaid Planning for Married Couples

As I stated, there's a lot of misinformation when it comes to Medicaid planning. It exists when planning for a married couple as well as a single person.

I had a case recently where the wife was suffering from dementia. The husband was at the point of having to put her in a facility. A financial planner I worked with over the years called me into the case. The attendees in the meeting were the financial planner, the husband who I will call Bill, and his stepdaughter who I will call Susie. Susie had spoken with a social worker who said she specialized in Medicaid. The social worker told Susie that her stepfather could keep $50,000 and it would be necessary to spend the rest in order to get his wife Medicaid qualified.

Susie seemed to accept the social worker's position due to the fact she said she specialized in the Medicaid field. To make sure Bill knew the facts his stepdaughter received was inaccurate, I showed him the Oregon Spousal Impoverishment Community Spouse Maximum Resource Standard, which proved he could have one-half of their assets up to $120,900 (this was in 2017). I have no idea where the social worker got the amount of $50,000.

When I did the plan, their assets were about $300,000. He was able to keep the $120,900, and I was able to preserve the rest. The moral of the story is to be careful who you get your information from because it could be costly. If Bill had taken the social worker's advice and spent down to $50,000, he would have suffered a $70,900 mistake.

When it comes to a married couple, asset-protection specialists can save pretty much all of the couple's assets. I will show you how in the case of Jim and Connie.

Case Study: Jim and Connie

Jim suffers from dementia, and Connie can no longer care for him. She recently had to place him in a memory-care facility. Jim is eighty-two, and Connie is seventy-nine.

The goal is to provide immediate Medicaid eligibility for Jim and sufficient income for Connie while preserving their assets.

Assets

Bank: $50,000
Investments: $200,000

Income

Connie: $1,200
Jim: $1,550

Nursing Home Bill: $7,500

The First Step is to Determine the Spend-Down Amount

The couple has $250,000 in assets. In 2017 Connie could have 1/2 of the 250,000 up to $120,900 (As of 2018 the community spouse can have 1/2 of assets up to $123,600.) Of their $250,000 Connie can have $120,900 and Jim can have $2,000. The balance of $127,100 has to be spent down.

The Second Step is Implement the Annuity Plan

The amount of money over what Jim and Connie can keep is $127,100. To preserve their assets and get Jim immediately Medicaid qualified, we put the excess $127,100 in a Medicaid Compliant Annuity. The key is to put the annuity in Connie's name and keep Jim off the policy. Connie is the sole owner and annuitant. Under Oregon rules, the annuity has to pay out within one year of Connie's life expectancy. Her life expectancy is 10.33 years, so we set up the annuity to pay out over 9.33 years. The annuity will pay $1,928 a month to Connie. The annuity income and Social Security provide her the monthly income she needs.

Again, the secret to this is to have Connie, the healthy spouse, as the owner of the policy and have the payments going to her to meet her income needs. Once we get Jim Medicaid qualified, the state never looks at Connie again. She can take the money and spend it on her monthly needs or rebuild her savings/investments. The bottom line is that the money is available to her for whatever she needs or wants.

The Third Step is to Apply for Medicaid

Since we converted the $127,100 from a spend-down asset to income, we can apply to the state for Jim's Medicaid qualification. Instead of paying $7,500 out of income and savings for Jim's care, they now pay only his Social Security of $1,550 minus $60.18 for his monthly allowance, creating a savings of $5,890.

Don't be misled to believe you have to spend down your savings to $2,000 to get Medicaid qualified. That simply is not the truth. Being misled can be very costly.

Spreading IRA taxes over time creating income for the healthy spouse

Some states don't allow this, but some do. If they do, it's a great asset-protection strategy. As many know, there can only be one owner on qualified money such as an IRA, 401(k), or 403(b). If the IRA is transferred from the owner, while still alive, to a spouse, another family member, or into an irrevocable trust, it will change ownership on the IRA and create a taxable event.

The good news is the IRA can help create immediate Medicaid qualification while benefiting the healthy spouse. There is a Medicaid rule called the "name on the check." This simply means the income belongs to the person whose name is on the check. In the case of an IRA owned by a disabled spouse, the IRA cannot be transferred, as mentioned, to the healthy spouse without the total value of the IRA being taxed. Many times, the IRA can be fairly large, and if it is transferred, it can be very expensive. This is usually not advised.

In this case, we are looking to get the disabled spouse Medicaid qualified. Under Oregon rules, the IRA has to be spent down (not in all states). So what do we do? We'll use a tax-saving strategy to get the impaired spouse Medicaid qualified immediately. We take out an IRA/annuity to pay over the life expectancy of the disabled spouse. We are therefore spreading out the taxes and helping meet the required minimum distribution (RMD) necessary when the disabled spouse reaches age seventy and a half.

If done correctly, the income from the annuity does not have to be paid to the facility. By putting on the annuity application that the IRA owner is irrevocably making the monthly annuity payment to the spouse, he or she can receive the income without affecting Medicaid eligibility. Remember that the spouse is healthy and can do whatever they want with the income. This protects the IRA from excessive taxes, and it does not have to pay for care. This little-known strategy is underutilized but very powerful.

CHAPTER 5

Pre-planning using long-term funding solutions

For those who want to stay financially independent and not fall victim to the high cost of long-term care, this chapter is for you. I've already covered Medicaid planning for those in crisis. The good news is Medicaid is still available, but that might not be the case in the future for baby boomers. Unless you have millions of dollars, chances are you will go broke if there is a need for long-term care in the future and Medicaid is not available. If you are relatively healthy, read on.

My experience is that men are pretty cavalier when it comes to long-term care. I was in a meeting years ago with a husband and wife who were both retired. We talked about long-term care and the need to be insured.

The husband said, "Dave, if I ever get in that situation, I have a gun."

First of all, his response was not really compassionate toward his wife and how that might affect her life.

I jokingly said, "Even if you have a gun, you will have to be able to find it."

We all had a pretty good laugh.

Many families are affected by dementia, including my family. The husband, being of sound mind, doesn't know what his situation will be if he needs care in the future. Chances are his wife will take care of him. However, if the husband doesn't see the need to insure against long-term care for himself, he should be compassionate—for his wife's benefit—and consider insurance for her.

Statistics show that when a man needs care, the wife becomes the caregiver until she no longer can. Men usually pass before their wives do. What about the surviving caregiving spouse? If she needs care in the future, who's going to step up for her quality of life? I have found parents do not want to be a burden on their children. They want to remain independent. If Medicaid is not available and the surviving spouse is not a millionaire, then what? I appeal to the men to make sure a plan is put in place for the benefit of their mates.

Even though people have homeowner's insurance, renter's insurance, health insurance, and life insurance, 90 percent of retirees don't insure against their greatest risk: long-term care.

Here are the 2016 stats:

- Death by house fire...1 in 1506
- Major car accident...1 in 102
- Odds of heart disease...1 in 6
- Risk of long-term care...1 in 1.43

What I'm about to share with you most people do not know these solutions exist. The pre-planning strategies are unique. Here are three that traditional long-term care insurance does not provide:

1. There will never be any premium increase.

2. In almost all cases you get what I call a money back guarantee meaning if you change your mind or something happens in your life and you don't need this type of insurance anymore, you will get a return of the money you put in the policy.

3. If you don't need long-term care, your heirs will receive a death benefit that many times will be income tax-free. Contractually your heirs will receive a death benefit if the money is not exhausted to pay for care. Also, if you only use a portion of the pool of money, the remaining balance will be paid to those of your choice. So if you don't use it, you won't lose it.

The Pension Protection Act (PPA)...Tax Free Money

In 2006, the government adopted the Pension Protection Act (PPA). It was put into effect in 2010, but very few people know about it. I just gave a presentation to a group of elder-law attorneys, and they had never heard of it. If I put several financial planners in a room and asked whether they'd ever heard of the Pension Protection Act, most—if not all—would say no. I know this because I've asked many of them randomly.

Because of the ten thousand baby boomers retiring daily, the government knows Medicaid will be very restricted and hard to qualify for—or it will be nonexistent for seniors in the future. They made the PPA available to motivate boomers to be able to self-pay by purchasing tax-advantaged insurance products if they should need care in the future.

Here is how it works. There is about $2 trillion owned annuities. The majority are owned by seniors. Many of these annuities have been owned for several years. The advantages they provide are a competitive rate of return along with tax deferral. The concept is the government is allowing us to use its money to build our savings through tax deferral.

Let's say a person purchased an annuity for $100,000 some years ago. It has grown to $200,000. If the individual should need a long-term care in the future, the $100,000 of tax deferral would come out first to pay for care, and it would be taxable. If a person owned a PPA annuity and needed long-term care, the entire $200,000 would come out tax-free.

That is quite an advantage and can save an individual a lot of money. As an independent agent not captive to an insurance company, I select the companies I think are best for my clients. I work with companies that have filed their annuities under the PPA. If an individual has an annuity that is not filed under the PPA, they can transfer their current annuity into a PPA tax-free. It just requires paperwork.

I will cover how to leverage the annuity to provide more long-term-care benefits if one should need care in the future. This strategy works well because 70 percent of seniors who own annuities pass away without touching them. Statistics show they will only tap the annuity if they need money for health care in the future. If this is the case, why not position it to provide tax savings along with more money if care is needed?

The PPA and Annuity Based Long Term Care

Individuals owning PPA-filed annuities can have long-term-care riders attached to the annuities that provide special tax advantages. The cash value of the annuity is used to pay the premiums on the long-term-care contract. There is no out-of-pocket payment to receive the long-term-care benefits. It is all done internally. The act also allows people who currently own annuities that are not PPA filed to transfer to a tax-favored PPA annuity. This is done by what is called a 1035 exchange. A 1035 exchange can be done if the annuity is nonqualified, meaning it is not an IRA. If it is an IRA, it can still be transferred income tax-free by way of a trustee-to-trustee transfer.

Case Study

Below is an example of how an annuity-based LTC plan can help someone. We will call the client Fred. Fred is seventy. He lives alone and suffers from type 2 diabetes and some other health challenges. Since Fred has diabetes and other health problems, he is not a good candidate for traditional long-term-care insurance.

However, by using an annuity long-term-care approach, taking advantage of the Pension Protection Act, he was able to get insured. He currently has a $200,000 annuity with a taxable gain of $100,000. The money is not qualified, so he can use a 1035 exchange strategy to transfer his $200,000 annuity into a PPA annuity. This gives him the advantage of tax-free money if he ever needs long-term care. By using a PPA annuity if he ever needs care, he will receive $520,000 in benefits. One of the great features of this strategy is these benefits will pay for home health care, assisted living, and nursing home care. As most people do, Fred wants to stay home as long as possible, and this approach gives him $520,000 of at-home-care benefits. Also, he does not have to worry about paying more premiums, which he will never have to do.

Fred has the $200,000 annuity, $350,000 from the sale of his business, and $45,000 in checking.

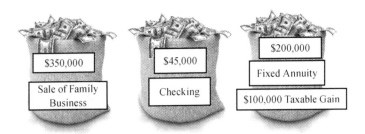

$350,000 — Sale of Family Business

$45,000 — Checking

$200,000 — Fixed Annuity — $100,000 Taxable Gain

Proposed

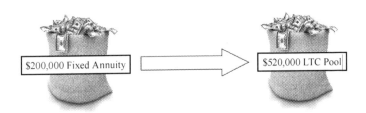

$200,000 Fixed Annuity → $520,000 LTC Pool

Hypothetically, by repositioning Fred's annuity, the following can happen:

- He retains his $200,000 in a tax-deferred fixed annuity.
- Fred receives an additional $320,000 in LTC benefits, totaling $520,000 tax-free.
- The benefits will pay for home care, assisted living, and nursing home.
- No additional premiums. He does not have to worry about premium increases.
- If he does not use his LTC benefits, his LTC benefits will grow as the annuity grows.
- If he doesn't use his benefits, or a portion, his heirs will receive a death benefit.

Asset-Based Strategy to Pay for Long-Term Care

Many people have rainy-day assets that they currently do not use to provide income to support their lifestyle. In most cases, these rainy-day assets are just that and will be used only if there is an unexpected cost such as health care. Statistics show that this money typically passes to their heirs. What if there's a way to have this money leveraged in case health care is needed and if it is never needed passed to your heirs—sometimes income-tax-free? When talking about the cost of health care for retirees, we are typically talking about long-term care.

Most people in retirement believe long-term-care insurance is an expense they don't need. They resist buying it because they lose it if they don't use it. All those premiums wasted.

In this section, I will show you how to provide protection for you and your family while also protecting it for your heirs if you never need long-term-care insurance.

As you read about asset-based long-term-care insurance, keep in mind this is not traditional long-term-care insurance. It is a creative strategy to protect you against the greatest risk you have of going broke. Once people know about this opportunity, a number of them take advantage of it because it only makes sense. If you're on the fence about protecting yourself against the long-term-care elephant in the room, ask yourself these questions:

What are your objections to buying long-term-care insurance even if you don't use it you don't lose it and you remain in control of the money?

What would motivate you to buy insurance to protect your assets, dignity, and independence?

What if Medicaid is no longer available and you do not have insurance or enough savings to private pay and you or your spouse need care? What would you do?

If you want to protect your assets, what I'm about to share with you will be important to you and your family.

To employ this strategy, money currently in bank accounts, annuities, and investments is shifted into a specially designed life insurance policy that is structured to pay for long-term care. The money is still yours—even when transferred to the life insurance policy. The life insurance is used to create a mechanism to pay for long-term care while also providing a death benefit to your beneficiaries if you never need long-term care. While most people in their lifetimes have life insurance or have purchased life insurance to protect their families against the loss of the main income earner, this is the same concept—except it is focused on protecting one's savings in case of long-term care. Again, life insurance to protect against the cost of long-term care is the same concept.

If you don't have a lump sum of money to shift over to life insurance, you can do like many people do when they purchase life insurance: make monthly payments. You can do the same in this situation.

The beauty of this approach is no one I know, including myself, wants to go to a nursing home. This is a way to stay at home as long as possible. The benefits from the asset-based long-term-care insurance pays for home health care, assisted living, adult foster care, and nursing home. It pays for long-term care if you have cognitive impairment or if you need help with two out of six activities of daily living, such as eating, dressing, walking, bathing, and other day-to-day activities.

There is peace of mind knowing that your money is safe and available for any other reason at any time. In most cases, you get a money-back guarantee. If you change your mind down the road or the government pays for care or whatever the scenario, you will get back the money you put into the policy. All you're doing is moving money from one account to another. This strategy can actually double or triple the amount of money you put in the policy. For example, $50,000 placed in the policy can provide as much as $250,000 in benefits. You can add a rider to the base policy that will pay lifetime benefits sometimes for only $2,500 a year. Premiums will never go up, and the payment is locked in.

It is simple math to know that $50,000 will last for about six months when the cost of care is $100,000 a year. That's a lot of personal savings that would be eaten up. You can see the leverage and benefit of this strategy. Obviously $250,000 is going to last a lot longer than $50,000. In addition, by using a life policy, filed under the PPA, all payments from the policy to pay for care are income tax-free.

If you don't want to purchase life insurance for asset protection, companies now have available fixed and index annuities with riders that perform the same way. Meet with a long-term-care financial specialist who can customize a plan for you.

HOW TO USE IRA MONEY TO FUND A LONG-TERM CARE STRATEGY FOR A SINGLE PERSON

In this day and age, many people are IRA rich and after-tax savings poor. In other words, they have a lot more qualified money than nonqualified money. IRA money is sometimes used to supplement income needs, and the rest gets set aside and warehoused in case health care is needed in the future.

Case Study

Jack is sixty-five and lives alone. He has recently been through a divorce. His main concern is if he needs long-term care in the future and how to pay for it. He has ample income.

He has $500,000 in an IRA. $150,000 is carved out and repositioned into an IRA-based annuity. The annuity will fund a life policy, providing Jack with long-term-care money should he need it later on in life. By doing this, he creates a death benefit of $255,000. Again, if he doesn't need long-term care, he doesn't lose his investment as he would with traditional long-term-care insurance. If he needs care, he will receive $5,132 a month for home health care, assisted living, adult care, or even skilled nursing home care.

Let's look at an example:

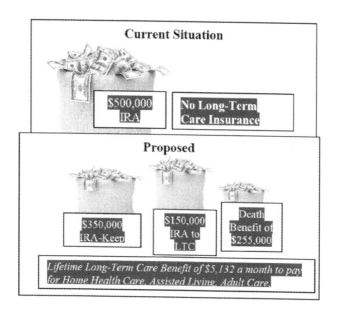

How to Use IRA Money to Fund a Long-Term Care Strategy for a Married Couple

Let's look at another example. How does an asset-based long-term-care policy benefit a married couple with most of their money in an IRA?

Judy is sixty, and Will is sixty-five. They are concerned about long-term care, but at this point, they have been fearful of purchasing a traditional long-term-care policy. They don't want to pay annual premiums, and they are concerned the premiums may increase in the future.

Will has $460,000 in his IRA. They currently do not need income from it. They are looking for a long-term-care funding strategy that will allow them to stay in control of their money and provide a death benefit to their children. If possible, they would like to be able to reduce the tax liability of the IRA if it does transfer to family. After discussing this strategy, it gave them peace of mind knowing they wouldn't fear any premium increases in the future, and if they didn't use the money—or if a portion of it was not consumed—their children would receive a death benefit. The death benefit may help offset the income tax liability from the IRA.

In addition to Will's IRA, they have $155,000 in savings. They also have income of $3,900 from pension and Social Security, which is adequate to meet their income needs. They transfer $240,000 from his IRA income tax-free to a second to die LTC asset-based policy.

Let's take a look at the strategy.

Will and Judy's Long-Term Care Solution

| $155,000 in saving & $220,000 IRA | $240,000 Into LTC Asset-Based Policy | LTC Benefits of $481,270 2nd To Die |

- $ 9,049 monthly benefit for life for both Judy and Will.
- Full refund of premium
- Covers home health, assisted living, adult care, nursing home
- At the death of both Will and Judy their children will receive a death benefit of $481,270

Traditional Long-Term Care Insurance

I think it's important to say I am not anti-traditional long-term-care insurance. As a past long-term-care instructor for the state of Washington, I taught the fundamentals of traditional long-term-care insurance. I have been involved in cases where it made the most sense for certain people. I believe it's an important arrow in the quiver of agents in the field when recommending the traditional approach to help people protect their money from the cost of care. I have a concern about how it is sold, which I will share with you. This chapter is about preplanning alternatives that are customized for seniors, and traditional long-term-care insurance is one of those options.

About 10 percent of seniors own long-term-care insurance. I believe this is for a few reasons:

- They don't feel they will need long-term-care insurance.

- They are not sure if premiums will increase, and if so, how much.
- They don't believe they will need long-term care and see insurance as an additional expense.
- If they don't use it, they lose it. If they never need care, they have wasted their money on paying premiums.

Many people who purchase insurance allow their policy to lapse because they're not sure they need it. The fact of the matter is they were sold a policy by a good salesman, but they weren't sure how the policy fit in their retirement picture.

I have a pet peeve when it comes to the sale of long-term-care insurance. If I fill a room with seniors who own long-term-care policies, most policies would be identical. They have the same exclusion period, benefit period, and benefit amount. Most would not have any inflation benefit. If I asked, "Do you think the person next you or anyone in the room has the same amount of savings, income, or goals, such as how much you would like to go to your heirs and how much you're willing to spend on long-term care?" They would agree they are all different. That being the case, why would their policies be the same? It doesn't make sense.

Many people who own policies are in for a rude awakening. If they don't need care for several years and their policy doesn't keep up with inflation, the cost of care might be more than their income and what the policy pays. They will have to apply for Medicaid and hope it is still available. This is why it's so important to have a customized plan.

As a long-term-care specialist, people ask me if they need a policy. To their surprise, I say, "I have no idea unless I run a cash-flow analysis. Otherwise, it is a shot in the dark. Without your goals and financial situation, I don't know if you can self-pay or if you need a policy. If you do need a policy, what are your specific needs such as the benefit amount and the benefit period?"

Along with seniors who would like to know if they need a policy are those who currently own one and would like to find out if it is right for them. Part of my practice is to run an analysis designed to determine if it fits within their retirement plan.

An example is a client who had long-term-care insurance before I started to work with her. I will call her Clara. Clara received a notice the insurance company was increasing her premiums by 40 percent. She asked me if she needed the policy.

I said, "Let me run the numbers, and I will let you know."

Based on her income and assets, while projecting a realistic cost of care—taking into consideration a higher expense than normal and her needing care for a longer period than average—I found she had adequate income and assets to self-pay.

I explained to her the downside. If she discontinued the policy, her assets identified to transfer to her heirs would be less than originally intended if she used her savings to pay for care. She would have to choose between paying the higher premium and having the inheritance distributed to family at her passing. She said she didn't want to pay the increase and decided to lapse the policy.

Why Long-Term Care Insurance is Important

Why buy long-term care insurance? I know of advisors who have said, "People don't need long-term care insurance because the government has a plan for us, and if we know how to qualify our worries are over." In my opinion, this advice is reckless! There are two good reasons why long-term care insurance is important:

1. No one knows what the state of government benefits will be in the future.

2. Long-term care insurance gives you more options

I am not just talking about traditional long-term care insurance but also the types under The Pension Protection Act.

Addressing "the government has a plan for us" (which is Medicaid), *no one knows what the state of government benefits will be in the future.* The rules will probably be different and more restrictive due to an influx of Baby Boomers retiring or Medicaid may not be available at all. Current debates focus on slowing the growth expenditures of entitlements *rather than how to improve long-term care protections for seniors.* Medicaid's long-term care services are a critical source of support for millions of citizens.

Slowing entitlement expenditures along with more restrictive medical and financial eligibility requirements *reinforces* the chance that Medicaid will not be available for those retirees who will need long-term care services in the future. Long-term care being the number one reason that elders become impoverished, the limitation of Medicaid has a direct impact on the well-being of retirees, especially those who are concerned about their spouse's financial security.

The facts are, *long- term care insurance gives you more options.* Anyone who has dealt with paying for long-term care would probably agree that those who can pay for services with their own money, or with money from an LTC policy, have more options than people who are on Medicaid. From my experience, facilities open their doors wide for people with money to pay, while those on public assistance may be faced with being placed on a waiting list (there is a way to get access to a facility and avoid being put on a waiting list). Why is that? In most situations, the facility receives less money from the state than from private pay clients.

Since most LTC facilities are owned by for profit companies, their "bottom line" is important if they are to stay in business. Naturally, the first priority for companies trying to make a profit is to fill their beds with private paying residents. Another advantage for those who have money is they can gain access to a facility by initially paying expenses either out of their own pocket or an insurance policy. Then after becoming a resident, they can go on Medicaid.

An LTC Policy Does Not Guarantee Better Care

While those with LTC policies have more care options than people on Medicaid, owning a policy does not guarantee better care. Unfortunately, many people who sell LTC insurance try to make Medicaid planning the scariest strategy that anyone can use for those in need of care. The story goes something like this: With Medicaid, your loved one will be shipped off to the ends of the earth, fed inedible leftover food, and put in a room that even a convicted killer would protest as a civil rights violation.

Here are the facts: Medicaid-licensed facilities cannot discriminate regarding the level of care provided to those clients who private pay and those clients who pay via Medicaid. Medicaid-licensed facilities have to abide by the rules under Medicaid. Is it possible for a facility to play games and make life a little less comfortable for a Medicaid patient? If motivated to make the bed available for a private-pay client, a facility's staff certainly could do that, but they risk a potential lawsuit if their actions are discriminatory.

Even a best-selling author added to this misconception regarding the quality of care in one of her books: "The spouse who needs long-term care is then sent to a Medicaid approved nursing home, which is not necessarily a place where you want to spend your last days."

I take issue with this generalized statement. First of all, people on Medicaid can receive care without having to go to a nursing home. Second, some people—due to health or affordability—do not have and cannot purchase long-term-care insurance. I think it is an injustice to scare those who have no alternative but to live in a Medicaid-licensed facility. My personal experience regarding the quality of care received by those on Medicaid—not what I read or what I heard from someone else—is quite different.

My father resided in a Medicaid-licensed Alzheimer's facility. His care was excellent. The facility did a good job of hiring people who cared about our elders. My family had no complaints. Like my father, my father and mother in-law also had a great living environment while on Medicaid. My in-laws, though on Medicaid, were moved by the good graces of the facility management to a larger apartment to better accommodate their needs.

Over the years, I have had several people referred to me who had modest savings and whose spouses needed care. In order to keep the healthy spouse financially independent, Medicaid was the best option. While I have clients who are very happy with the care their loved ones have received in Medicaid-licensed facilities, other clients are not happy with the care their spouses received—even though they were paying out of their own pockets.

From my experience, the standard of care depends largely on the management of the facility and the involvement of the patient's family. Ultimately, it has a lot to do with the homework a family has done prior to placing a loved one in a facility and how active the family is in the ongoing care of their loved one. I recommend visiting any facility—whether it is a Medicaid-licensed facility or a place that only takes private pay clients. Do your homework *before* you decide.

Here is the bottom line: Buying a long-term-care policy does not guarantee better care for you or your family member. It does provide more options and easier access to some facilities. In my opinion, painting a scary picture of Medicaid in order to sell long-term-care insurance is self-serving for the agent/adviser. Long-term-care insurance should be purchased based on need and the fact that we don't know what the state of Medicaid will be in the future—and because long-term-care insurance gives us more options. But since not everyone can qualify due to health issues or the inability to afford LTC insurance, shame on us if we try to scare them or ignore their needs

The First Step Before Buying a Policy

In order to find out if you need insurance, a financial analysis should be completed. Some will find they need it, and some will find that they do not. The following questions should be addressed in your financial plan to determine if you need long-term-care insurance, and if so, how much.

- o What is the projected cost of care with inflation factored in?
- o What is the risk exposure? Do you currently have enough income and assets to be financially independent if you should need long-term care?
- o What assets (if any) would you like to protect for the next generation? Which assets are you willing to spend on care?
- o What income will go toward paying for care, and what income will need to go to a spouse (if there is a spouse)?

o Can the policy premiums be paid for with current cash flow—or is a creative payment plan more appropriate?

o Will you be able to afford premiums if they increase in the future—or is it better to pay the premiums over a short time period?

o Is it more efficient to go with a hybrid policy that guarantees no premium increase and if the benefits are not exhausted it provides a death benefit for your heirs?

After a thorough analysis of a client's financial situation and determination of goals and objectives, a qualified financial adviser can determine what's known as *insurance efficiency*. Insurance efficiency is reached by not having too much insurance, which nobody wants, or having too little, which creates unwanted risk. From there, a qualified adviser can better determine what benefit amount is needed, what elimination period is best, what benefit period makes sense, what inflation factor should be used, and what special features (if any) make sense.

I have found that a person is more likely to keep a policy that fits their personal needs, is affordable (paying for it doesn't change one's lifestyle), and is understandable in terms of the role it plays in helping provide financial security. After the analysis, if the plan shows that you need it, the next step is to choose the right policy for you.

Important Policy Features

Long-term-care policy features can fill an entire book. I will concentrate more on what I believe are critical issues of choosing a policy and stick to the basics. While my approach to long-term care is holistic (how it integrates with all aspects of a person's financial life), for those of you who want a more in-depth look at long-term-care policy features (which I would encourage), there are excellent books on the subject.

Daily Benefit

The daily benefit refers to how much the policy will pay for long-term-care services per day. As I wrote earlier, I am floored by the number of people who have policies that pay the same daily benefit. This eats at me! It is nearly impossible to find two families with the same income, assets (savings and investments), expenses, same health, and same age. Why in the world would they have the same daily benefit?

My findings lead me to believe that the salesperson's focus was on selling whatever policy he or she could—even if it didn't meet the needs of the client. I find no fault with the client since most assume the person selling the policy knows what they are doing. Obviously, the policy was sold to them rather than them buying a product that was needed to add security to their life. Once again, if the client doesn't know why they have it and how it fits into their financial life, many will stop paying premiums down the road, ultimately wasting their money.

Do not choose a daily benefit until you have considered other important financial factors that are unique to you and your family.

Benefit Period

People often mistakenly think the benefit period refers to how many years they are covered after buying the policy. This is a misunderstanding. The benefit period refers to the time between when the policy starts paying benefits and when it stops. For example, a person age sixty-five purchases a policy with a five-year benefit period. Let's also say that she needs care at age eighty. If she meets the policy requirements, she will receive benefits for five years assuming she continues to live. In this case, she received benefits from age eighty to age eighty-five. When choosing a benefit period, apply the same criteria used to choose the correct daily benefit.

Elimination or Waiting Period

The elimination period, which can also be called the waiting period, refers to the number of days one has to pay out of pocket for care before the insurance company starts to shell out. The elimination period begins the day you qualify for benefits under the policy. A ninety-day elimination period is common, and I usually advise my clients to take it because most people can pay out of pocket for care through ninety days without causing a problem. Choosing a shorter elimination period such as thirty, forty-five, or sixty days just increases the premiums. I would rather see my clients put the extra money in their pockets than give their money to the insurance company.

Inflation Protection

Health care costs are increasing annually at an alarming rate. What does that mean to people purchasing long-term-care policies? Make sure what you are buying now will do what you think it will years down the road when you are most likely to need care. If you do not, you might be wasting money. You might be better off not buying a policy at all.

As an example, let's say Mrs. Thomas takes out a policy today for a $130 daily benefit. She doesn't have an inflation rider to counteract the increase in the cost of care in the future. By the time she actually needs care, the daily cost is $330 a day. If she doesn't have enough money from her assets, income, and policy to pay for care, she could end up on public assistance. Unfortunately, some agents have sold policies without taking into account the need for inflation coverage because adding on the cost of inflation, would potentially kill the sale.

When choosing an inflation option, you can select *simple* or *compound*. Simple is cheaper because it grows slower and is less expensive for the insurance company. If your original daily benefit is $100, and the inflation rate is 5 percent, each year you multiply $100 by 5 percent and add that amount to the original $100. In this example, after ten years, you have a daily benefit of $145. The compound interest option is more expensive because your benefit grows more over time than with the simple option. With the compound option, each year you multiply by the accumulated amount—in this case, 5 percent—as opposed to the original $100. After ten years, you have a daily benefit of $163.

To reduce the cost of a policy, instead of paying the extra for the inflation benefit, some people pay for a daily benefit that is much greater than they need today. The thought is that when care is needed down the road, one will have a larger benefit. While this option seems plausible, if a miscalculation is made and care isn't needed until later in life than projected, there may not be enough of a benefit to pay the bill. Most companies give you the option of increasing your benefit amount in the future instead of taking out an inflation option today. This choice is usually very expensive and oftentimes doesn't pencil out.

The Choice of An Indemnity (per diem) or Reimbursement Policy

Depending on the insurance company, you can choose between being paid back for expenses (reimbursement policy) or receive a specified dollar amount to be paid to you even if you have no out-of-pocket expense (indemnity policy). While the indemnity policy provides more independence, allowing you to spend the money however you would like, be careful to use the money wisely. Otherwise, you may find that you have prematurely exhausted your benefit.

Indemnity policies are fairly rare and can be more expensive because the insurance company has less control and may have to pay money to the policyholder over a shorter time period than with a reimbursement policy. The choice between these two options should be based on need and comfort.

Check out your long-term care policy carrier

Many insurance companies sell LTC policies. Here are some things you should know before choosing a carrier:

o   How does their cost of insurance compare with other companies that sell a comparable policy? Be careful about choosing the company with the lowest premium. Low premiums can be a result of a company's willingness to underwrite people with questionable health in order to attract business. If you choose such a carrier, you may be paying a higher premium in the future if the insurance company hasn't fairly priced their risk exposure.

o   You may pay premiums for several years prior to applying for benefits from an insurance company. Therefore, the financial strength of the company is very important. When you need your money, you want the company to be in business and be able to pay your claims. What is the financial strength of the companies you're considering? You can find the ratings for the insurance company you're considering by contacting the ratings companies by phone, searching on the internet, or going to your local library. Many insurance companies have their ratings on their websites and in their printed marketing materials. Your state's insurance department may be able to provide you with this information or direct you where to find it.

o Experience varies between companies. Some carriers have exited the long-term-care market for various reasons. Choose a company that has been in the long-term-care market for several years and has a track record you can check out.

o What is its claim-paying history? Is the company slow to pay claims? Does it have a track record of claim denial? You won't usually get this information from the insurance carrier. Check with the Department of Insurance in your state to find out if the company you're considering has had complaints regarding these issues. This is another reason to consider companies that have strong ratings and have been selling long-term-care policies for several years.

o In what condition does the insured have to be in before the insurance company will start paying benefits? Companies vary on what triggers benefits. From my experience, what triggers benefits is something often overlooked by policy owners. You don't want to assume that money will be there if you need it only to find out later that the policy is more restrictive than you thought.

Some Long-term care Insurance Don'ts

o Don't buy an LTC policy because you believe it is a tax write-off. The policy should be purchased to help protect your financial independence and stand on its own merit. Insurance agents and the media will talk about LTC policies being tax-qualified and, therefore, tax-deductible. Many policyholders are surprised to find they don't get a penny of their tax dollars returned by the government.

o Don't buy a policy just because your friend has one. You may pay for something that makes no sense for you to own, resulting in wasting money that could be invested to help create more security.

o Don't buy policy add-ons (bells and whistles) unless you know you need them. You may end up adding a lot of cost, increasing your premiums for no good reason.

Your State May Allow You to Buy a Partnership Policy

After DRA 2005, more states adopted partnership policies. While partnership policies can still cost the state money, it is a much better option than Medicaid paying the entire bill. To encourage the purchase of long-term-care policies, people who buy these policies can protect some of their assets that would otherwise need to be spent down in order to qualify for Medicaid. For example, to qualify for public assistance (Medicaid) in your state, you can keep $2,000 in your name. If you purchase a partnership policy with a benefit amount of $300,000, you would be able to keep $302,000 ($300,000 plus $2,000) and still qualify for Medicaid. This strategy can be effective for a couple of reasons:

- You can reduce the amount of coverage, which reduces your premiums.
- The extra money can provide quality-of-life purchases while receiving Medicaid benefits. In most states, Medicaid does not pay for extras such

as outings with family, extra food for your room, cable television, telephone, or new bedsheets. The extra $300,000 can help pay for some of your extra needs while you are still receiving public assistance.

- Most people do not reside in a care facility longer than two and a half years. The longer someone can private pay, the less cost the state will have to pick up. For those who have policies that will take them past two and a half years, there is a good chance the state will not have to pay for any of the care.

Note: Before buying a partnership policy, check to find out the particulars for the state you live in.

CHAPTER 6

Legal tools needed to protect your assets and estate plan

Your attorney puts together an estate plan: a will, a trust, a power of attorney, and other documents. Why do we put together such a plan? After working hard, upon your passing, you want your money to go to those you choose to receive it.

It is common to use what is lawful to save taxes, time, and expenses by setting up a customized financial and estate plan. It makes sense! A correct plan can allow you to control what happens to your money from the grave. Some use their plans to dictate the actions of family members. As an example, we may use a trust to inspire our children or grandchildren to get an education. The trust is structured to pay out a certain amount of money to our loved one (or ones) only if they graduate from college. We might demand they receive a certain grade point average before receiving any of our hard-earned savings. We can require them to sit on a philanthropic board and do good things for the community—or else receive no money from the trust.

But what if after all the planning, family meetings, and attorney meetings, along with paying the attorney to provide all of the necessary documents, you failed to take into account one important estate-planning consideration? If you have no money, your estate plan is worthless. Money, time, and planning can be compromised. What am I referring to?

As I have mentioned, the number one reason people become impoverished in retirement is the cost of long-term care. What if you have an extra $100,000 a year in long-term-care expenses you never planned on? Because of this additional expense, what if your estate and financial plan was financially diminished or gone altogether?

Adding long-term-care planning can help you maintain its value and allow you to control your money in the manner in which you designed. By employing the Pension Protection Act and other government-approved strategies, you can move toward protecting your plan and your money. This can be accomplished without any additional expenses. If you haven't done this type of planning, you may want to consider it.

The following tools will help keep your financial and estate plan intact. I will address the following:

- trusts
- wills
- financial power of attorney
- health care power of attorney

Trusts

What is the benefit of a trust? The various types of trusts include special needs trusts, living trusts (sometimes called revocable trusts), and irrevocable trusts. To focus on the goal of asset protection, I will address these three types of trusts.

Special Needs Trust

A special needs trust (SNT) is commonly used in the case where a person is disabled. A special needs trust is more easily funded when the person is under age sixty-five. I will discuss an SNT for those over age sixty-five. A person on Medicaid cannot have more than $2,000 in their name without risking losing their benefits. Therefore, it is imperative to make sure the Medicaid recipient is not the beneficiary on any life insurance or other assets. This means the family has to make sure any wills, assets, and life insurance policies do not identify the disabled person as a beneficiary.

The benefit of setting up a SNT is if the healthy spouse predeceases the disabled spouse or the family wants to leave assets to the disabled person—again making sure it is not left outright—the money would go into a SNT so the impaired person can benefit from assets to provide them with quality of life without disrupting their Medicaid benefits. This is a complex trust and a complex process that varies from state to state. It is important to meet with an elder-law attorney to discuss the process and make sure the rules are met within that state.

Living Trusts

Living trusts or revocable living trusts have become very popular over the years. Unlike a will that goes through probate, the assets in the trust can pass directly to the heirs. It is also more difficult to dispute a trust than a will. The disadvantages to a will are it goes through probate, which can take a lot of time because the assets have to be retitled. It is also made public to allow creditors to claim against the estate of the deceased.

There are fees paid to tax advisers, the cost of the court proceedings, and the time it takes to conclude. A client was upset because the tax person, the court, and others received their pay first—and the heirs had to wait to get their money. One case actually took more than six months. This is one reason why living trusts have become so popular. The money from the trust can be distributed quickly to the heirs, it is not made public, and it can be very valuable if one becomes disabled.

More people are using living trust to preserve their legacies. A person can set up a trust that stipulates no payments will be made to heirs unless they meet the trust's requirements. As an example, the grantor may require his or her grandchildren to graduate from college with a certain grade point average. If the grandchild does not meet this requirement, they will not receive any money from the trust. More people who have built wealth are doing this. History shows that the wealth is usually gone by the third generation. It's not uncommon for the trust to require an heir to be active in the community by helping others to receive finances from the trust.

Regarding disability, if a person establishes a living trust, and is therefore the grantor of the trust, they are usually their own trustee. It is advisable they have a successor trustee. If the grantor becomes disabled, the successor trustee can step in and take over managing the trust. Security is provided due to the fact the successor trustee has to follow the grantor's wishes established in the trust at the time it was drafted. Because the trust is revocable—and therefore flexible—the establisher or grantor can modify it any time he or she desires.

One thing that is sometimes overlooked is that assets have to be retitled in the name of the trust. It is basically empty and therefore has no authority over the assets if they are not in the trust. This means the assets will not flow as designed by the trust; therefore, the will of the grantor will not be served. In addition, the successor trustee will not be able to manage the trust in case of a disability of the grantor.

For purposes of Medicaid qualification, the assets in a living trust are subject to spend down. A living trust does not protect assets in case there is a need for Medicaid benefits. For the purposes of Medicaid planning, a living trust provides no advantages other than the successor trustee being able to access funds to help protect the grantor by way of professional guidance.

Another benefit of a living trust is people find it easier to access a disabled spouse's accounts that are held in his or her name. Even if a person has a financial power of attorney, which I will talk about, sometimes financial institutions, especially banks, will question the power of attorney. The bank usually runs it past their attorneys. They typically do not do that with a living trust. Ultimately, most banks will accept the power of attorney without getting a client's attorney involved, but a living trust can provide less hassle.

Irrevocable Trusts

Unlike a revocable trust, where the grantor can make modifications to the trust—and for tax purposes, it still belongs to the establisher of the trust—an irrevocable trust is irrevocable. Once established, it becomes a separate entity with its own tax ID number. An irrevocable trust is usually drafted to minimize estate taxes and control the grantor's legacy.

Irrevocable trusts are commonly used by elder-law attorneys for Medicaid planning purposes. As of 2005, the Deficit Reduction Act (DRA) extended the Medicaid look-back period from three to five years for individuals. When there is a relatively large amount of money being transferred out of the estate, an irrevocable trust is commonly used. When I say a relatively large amount of money, I'm not talking about millionaires. I do not believe in putting millionaires on Medicaid. In most cases, there are exceptions; millionaires can usually private pay when in need of long-term care.

In the right circumstances, I think an irrevocable trust, for asset protection, is typically a good option. Every case should be looked at individually to determine the best plan and strategy.

When money is transferred, it can create a period of ineligibility for Medicaid benefits. The disqualification period is usually best served by using an annuity to pay for the disabled person's care. If money is transferred to the adult children, the annuity provides a level of security. By putting some of the money into an irrevocable trust, if drafted correctly by the attorney, money can be paid out of the trust for the benefit of the disabled person. This works well when the cost of care increases beyond the client's income and the money is coming from the annuity. The trustee can dip into the trust to pay the needed additional money. This flexibility usually provides additional security for the disabled client.

Financial Powers of Attorney

Many married people believe they have access to their spouse's account even if it is not held jointly and is in the spouse's individual name. This is not the case, which brings us to the financial power of attorney.

I am currently working on a case referred to me by an elder-law attorney. The spouse is disabled and only sixty-five years old. I recently had a case where the disabled spouse was only fifty-six years old. Both are way too young. I know from personal experience this is an insidious and devastating disease.

In the case I am working on, the husband does not have a power of attorney. His disabled spouse has an IRA that obviously has to be in her name. However, since he cannot access the funds, we are not able to achieve asset protection. Since he does not have a power of attorney, his attorney who referred me into the case has to go to court to secure a guardianship. This can cost my client $2,000 or $3,000, which delays the process of getting his wife Medicaid qualified.

The durable power of attorney is an important document for any estate plan, but it may be even more important for those planning on obtaining Medicaid eligibility.

Establishing a durable power of attorney is a way to protect yourself should the day come when you are no longer able to make important decisions due to illness, injury, or the potentially devastating effects of dementia. The person creating the power is called the principal who nominates a person or persons named the attorney-in-fact to act on your behalf in ways that are specifically authorized in the document creating the power. The power becomes effective if and when the principal (you) becomes incapacitated, allowing the principal to dictate the terms of how you will be cared for as well as how your estate will be handled should the need arise.

This document is important to draft in advance of actually needing long-term care. As I mentioned regarding my client who needs a guardianship due to not having a durable power of attorney drafted ahead of time, his Medicaid plan was delayed. Suppose, for instance, that you and your family abhor the idea of seeing your life's savings drained away by the costs of medical care later in life (who doesn't?). However, you think you are currently too young and healthy to transfer your property to trusts or take advantage of the other options available to preserve your assets while obtaining Medicaid eligibility. In this case, the best course of action may be to craft your estate plan using a durable power of attorney so that your attorney-in-fact will have the powers necessary to execute your plans at a later date.

If properly drafted, a durable power of attorney can allow your agent, when the need arises, to make the transfers that may allow you to qualify for Medicaid. If you become disabled and are unable to execute your estate plan, your agent can still be directed to act on your behalf, thereby giving you an assurance that your wishes will be respected and your interests protected.

Health Care Power of Attorney

Most of us have heard of a living will. How is a health care power of attorney different—and why is one important? A health care power of attorney goes further than a living will. The big restriction with a living will is that it only applies if you are terminally ill, permanently unconscious, or in another similar condition as defined by state law. If you are only temporarily unconscious or otherwise unable to communicate, but are not terminally ill, in a permanent vegetative state, or an end-stage condition, a living will is of no use. You need a health care power of attorney to cover such a situation.

A health care power of attorney is a document in which you designate someone to be your representative, or agent, in the event you are unable to make or communicate decisions about all aspects of your health care. In the most basic form, this document merely says, "I want this person to make decisions about my health care if I am unable to do so."

The person you are choosing to be your agent who you are trusting to make medical decisions on your behalf if you can't make them for yourself. You should think carefully about who you want to assume this responsibility. This is an important decision because the person you choose may be deciding whether or not life-support measures will be in your best interests or determining exactly how your personal and religious values would impact other treatments.

A living will can accompany your health care power of attorney—or the two may be combined into one document. Other various matters may be included, such as designating a primary physician, the donation of body organs, and who you would like appointed as your legal guardian if the need arises.

Commonly, people choose to have a separate living will to give the agent some guidance. You can design your health care documents to be as broad as possible, or it can limit the type of decisions your agent can make. If you do not have a living will or do not make any type of statements in your health care power of attorney about your desires, you are leaving it up to the person you designate to decide what you would want in a certain situation. It can be a great help to your agent if your documents provide clear direction.

Should a senior put an adult child on their financial accounts?

It seems common practice for a senior to put an adult child on their financial accounts, usually their bank accounts. Sometimes this is done for convenience. It is also done as a way to help protect assets. The senior may be trying to establish an inheritance if something should happen to him or her.

I am not a fan of this process. If the adult child is sued or goes through a divorce, the parent's money may be at risk. In addition, for Medicaid planning purposes, the state views the money as belonging to the parent even if the account is set up as joint.

Payable-on-death (POD) accounts offer one of the easiest ways to transfer money to heirs outside of probate. All you need to do is fill out a simple form, provided by the bank, naming the person you want to inherit the money at your death.

As long as you are alive, the person you named to inherit the money in a payable-on-death account has no rights to it. You can spend the money, name a different beneficiary, or close the account. At your death, the beneficiary simply goes to the bank, shows proof of death and his or her identity, and collects whatever funds are in the account. The probate court is never involved.

If you and your spouse have a joint account, when the first spouse dies, the funds in the account will probably become the property of the survivor—without probate. If you add a POD designation, it will take effect only when the second spouse dies.

For annuities, life insurance, and IRAs, you can designate a beneficiary. It will pass outside of probate and can be changed at any time.

CHAPTER 7

Finding a trusted advisor who can help

B ack in the eighties, I told my parents I was transitioning from the restaurant business into the financial-services business.

My mother said, "You don't want to get into money management because people can be very emotional when it comes to their savings."

After thirty-one years in the business, I agree. When I started with American Express in 1986, I studied investing voraciously. I would read *Forbes* and pick up every book I could on the subject. I learned even the pros don't always get it right. Many times, they don't see the recession coming or the downturn in the market. Whenever I hear people say they are playing the stock market or investing in the stock market, I cringe. The appropriate way to invest is researching companies and studying their income and balance sheets.

The fact of the matter is it's not investing in the market—it's investing in companies, which is totally different.

Nobody has ever been able to consistently predict the stock market. Warren Buffett didn't get rich investing in the market. His wealth has come from investing in companies. As matter of fact, Warren Buffett's mentor, Benjamin Graham, became wealthy buying businesses selling for less than their tangible assets. He didn't even take into consideration their earnings, which is the focus of Wall Street. Warren Buffett has taken that to a new level. He *does* consider the strength of the company and its positioning in the marketplace. For people who want to learn about investing, I highly recommend Benjamin Graham's *The Intelligent Investor* and *Security Analysis*.

Although I am passionate about the investment process, as I have helped many clients with portfolio design, my focus has been on asset protection. Because of my years of experience, I am confident in the outcome when I say I can help somebody protect their assets. I give everyone I work with a money-back guarantee. If I can't accomplish what I say I can, I will return their fee. In eighteen years of Medicaid planning, I have not returned one fee.

I look back to 1999 and still scratch my head about how I got into asset protection as my vocation. I'm glad I did since it is very rewarding. Over the past eighteen years, I have dedicated my practice to helping people protect their life savings when faced with a high cost of long-term care. Again, this is the number one reason why people become impoverished in retirement. Spending all of one's savings because of the high cost of long-term care is a lot greater risk than achieving a nominal return on an investment or even a negative return. Unless an investor is a gambler, investing is not going to wipe out a person's savings, but long-term care can and does.

No matter who you choose as an adviser—investment person, financial planner, or insurance agent—you are trusting them to take your best interests into account. As a Certified Financial Planner (CFP®), I am obligated to act as a fiduciary to put my client's interest before mine.

Anyone can call themselves a financial planner. There are now more promotions and television commercials addressing the benefits of working with a Certified Financial Planner. A Certified Financial Planner has studied and passed six very difficult educational classes. The last I heard, the passing percentage was only 54 percent.

Financial Planning: Process and Environment

- communication techniques
- ethics
- education planning and funding
- time-value-of-money concepts
- financial planning applications
- regulatory issues
- legal and economic environment for financial planning

- Personal Financial Planning- Comprehensive Case Analysis

- o Retirement
- o Investment
- o Risk management
- o Income tax
- o Employee benefits
- o General principles

- Fundamentals of Insurance Planning

  - o Focuses on the role of planning for insurance needs. Covers basic concepts in risk management and insurance, insurance industry operations, legal principles pertaining to this industry, and regulation of insurers. Examines social insurance, life insurance and annuities, medical and disability income insurance, long-term care insurance and personal property and liability insurance. Concludes with an overview of commercial property and liability insurance and a case study.

- Investments

  - o Risk analysis, risk and return computations
  - o Risk reduction through diversification
  - o Expected returns of various investments
  - o Nature of securities markets and investment companies
  - o Tax issues in investing
  - o Issues in the practice of portfolio management
  - o Examples of ethical and practical investment considerations

- o Planning for Retirement Needs
- o Qualified plans, SEPs, SIMPLEs and 403(b) plans
- o Nonqualified deferred compensation plans
- o Practical knowledge needed for choosing the best retirement plan, especially for the small business, and designing a plan that will meet a client's needs
- o Individual retirement planning including IRAs and Roth IRAs, Social Security benefits, saving for retirement and planning for retirement plan distributions

- Fundamentals of Estate Planning

  - o Nature, valuation transfer, administration, and taxation of property
  - o Gratuitous transfers of property outright or with trusts, wills and powers of appointment
  - o Use of the marital deduction
  - o Valuation of assets
  - o Buy-sell agreements
  - o Client interview/fact finding
  - o Ethical standards
  - o Development of personal estate plans

- Income Taxation

  - o Gross income, exclusions from gross income
  - o Deductions
  - o Tax credits
  - o Capital gains and losses

- o Taxation of life insurance
- o Taxation of annuities
- o Entity taxation of partnerships, LLCs, corporations, and proprietorships

When I applied, the requirement was two years of financial planning experience before I could receive my certified financial planner designation.

The benefit of working with a certified financial planner is having an adviser who has experience in the field and a strong knowledge base, and follows the ethics of the Certified Financial Planning Board. If a CFP® does not follow or is outside of the ethics standards, he or she can lose their license and designation.

If you're dealing with a long-term-care crisis for an aging loved one who is in a care facility—nursing home, adult foster care, assisted-living, continual-care community, or other facility—the first thing is to find a long-term-care specialist, such as myself, who is qualified to put together a plan in conjunction with an elder-law attorney to help protect your family's assets.

The vast majority of financial planners do not have specialized knowledge and experience in this field. Most financial planners provide retirement planning and investment options. Many of my referrals come from financial planners who are not versed in asset protection. A long-term care/asset protection specialist is able to guide you through the right process by clearly defining your loved one's care needs and providing a comprehensive analysis and evaluation, resulting in a comprehensive plan. The plan would include an inventory of assets (savings and investments), income (such as Social Security, pensions, or annuity income), and an income tax evaluation. While I do not give income tax advice, I do look at the income tax liability if we need to move money into a Medicaid-compliant annuity to protect savings.

Important Considerations When Choosing an Advisor

Find out if the adviser has had any ethics violations, license revocations, or suspensions. If the adviser is securities licensed, you can check their status by contacting the Financial Industry Regulatory Authority (FINRA) at finra.org. If an adviser is insurance licensed, check with the Department of Insurance in your state. If they have professional designations, you can check with the issuing organization. The more common designations have codes of ethics and require various levels of education. To check about a certified financial planner, contact cffpinfo.com or 800-237-9990. To check on a chartered life underwriter (CLU) or chartered financial consultant (ChFC), contact the American College at 888-263-7265.

If creating a financial plan is free of charge, keep in mind the old saying that there is no free lunch. In order for the adviser to make a living, you will have to buy something. A financial plan should stand on its own without representing any financial products. I believe you can get objective advice from someone who receives income only from commissions, but you must understand that's how the adviser's compensation is determined before your plan is created. Take to heart this wise saying: Free advice may be the most expensive advice you ever receive.

Choose an adviser with the right focus for you. When clients come to me, I tell them my area of expertise and how I work with clients. If they are looking for someone with a different focus or expertise, I'll guide them to an adviser who is more suited to their needs. Finding an adviser who is right for you might take some research and a few interviews.

Realize that any savings or investment plans you get involved in will always have an upside and a downside. No investment or savings plan is perfect. Your adviser should make sure you know the positives and negatives of any financial decisions you make. For example, when you put your money in a certificate of deposit, you're giving up interest on your money for security. If you invest in stocks, you're giving up safety for the potential of a better return. Understand what you are investing in. You should be solving a problem and not creating one.

Never loan money to a financial adviser or invest in a firm that's owned or controlled by the adviser. These are ethics violations. If you are ever asked to do either, you should report the adviser. If the adviser is an insurance agent, call the Department of Insurance in your state or contact FINRA if he or she is a registered representative. Then find another adviser.

Your adviser should focus on you. Your adviser should provide you with all the information necessary to make an informed decision, and you should never feel rushed.

If they are trying to rush you, they are probably working in their own interest—and not yours. It may be necessary to meet several times where you ask questions and they guide and educate you before you feel comfortable making a decision. Your adviser should be willing to spend the time to accomplish that objective.

Work with an adviser who has many arrows in their quiver. Isn't it funny how an adviser who sells only whole life insurance, for instance, will discover that someone who needs a financial product needs whole life insurance? Whole life might be right for you—or it might be wrong—but your adviser should be working on your behalf to find the right product and right product manufacturer to meet your needs. If your adviser has only a hammer, then everything looks like a nail. Don't get nailed with bad advice. Make sure the person you entrust with your money is looking out for your needs.

You must be willing to share your personal financial information with your adviser if you expect them to do a quality job for you. They must be privy to your tax status, investment objectives, risk tolerance, time horizon, and other information specific to your situation. Otherwise, their recommendations may not be suitable for your needs.

Make sure your adviser is qualified to help you. The new retirement culture calls for specialized experience and education. They should have experience and expertise in the following areas:

o   long-term care

o   asset allocation
o   how to help ensure income for life
o   tax-saving efficiencies
o   legal tools
o   ownership and beneficiary designations to protect assets and survivor income

Interview the prospective adviser before you decide to hire them. You will be working closely together and sharing your personal information. Unless you are confident that the adviser is right for you, do not hesitate to keep looking. Your financial well-being may depend upon it.

How about doing your own financial planning? Some personal finance software packages, magazines, and self-help books can give you the fundamentals of how to do your own financial planning. However, you may decide to seek help from a professional financial planner if:

- You need expertise you don't possess in certain areas of your finances. For example, a planner can help you evaluate the level of risk in your investment portfolio or determine the rate of return you need to stay financially independent.
- You or your spouse needs long-term care—and you want to know the smartest way to pay for it.
- You want to get a professional opinion about the financial plan you developed for yourself.
- You don't feel you have the time to spare to do your own financial planning or need a second opinion.
- You have an immediate need or unexpected life event such as a death, inheritance, or major illness.

- You are not sure you are doing things right and need guidance.
- You are not sure you own your assets correctly to protect yourself from disinheritance, major illness, or transferring your money to your loved ones without unnecessary cost, delay, and taxes.

CHAPTER 8

Where to go from here

*"Always plan ahead. It wasn't raining
when Noah built the ark."*

Richard C. Cushing

*"For the great gain of education is not
knowledge but action."*

Herbert Spencer

A couple who I will call Phil and Lois came to see me. Having never met them before, as with all of my introductory meetings, I was there to listen and find out how they were hoping I could help them. Phil had a look of worry on his face. He looked like a man under stress. As he and Lois spoke with me, I was starting to understand why. Phil was raised in a culture that strongly believed the man should be responsible for the family's finances. He worked hard at his profession as a plant manager and had been a good provider. Phil's expression showed the strain of entering a new phase in his life: transitioning from working to pay the bills to investing to provide a comfortable lifestyle for him and Lois. Phil worried if he made a mistake at this time in their lives, they could not earn back their savings they'd worked so hard to accumulate. A misstep would be catastrophic.

This new hat was obviously uncomfortable for Phil. Adding to his stress, they had recently attended an investment seminar that raised more questions than answers. Unfortunately, Phil and Lois left the seminar confused about how to navigate the future. The seminar speakers talked about an array of investment options that made their heads spin. In addition, they told me they didn't understand some of the investment terms that were used. They attended the seminar because they simply wanted to invest their money for retirement—not to take a class on a multitude of investment terms.

Phil and Lois were hoping I could provide clarity and reassurance. They wanted a simple solution to a complex process. I told them the same thing I have shared with you in this book; without a plan, they would be shooting in the dark and so would their adviser. Without a plan to direct them along with the person or team assisting, they might as well flip a coin and hope for the best. They were about to go down an investment trail and make the mistake that so many investors make: they were falling in the trap of investing their money before investing their time in mapping out their future. Once they map out where they are and where they want to go, they can take action to get there with confidence. They must determine their needs and then then choose the right strategy to meet them—and not the other way around.

In *Age Power*, Dr. Ken Dychtwald said, "Lacking proactive planning, many elders wind up depleting their life savings—and their children's inheritance—as they tumble into poverty." Who wants that? So why don't more people plan? Don't get mad at me, but I have to put much of the blame on us guys for not planning our financial futures. Either we don't want a financial adviser nosing in our business—or we believe we can do it ourselves (even though 78 percent of us don't do it). Then again, we are the ones who think we can drive to any destination and don't even need a map, right? I haven't done the research, but I don't think it is a stretch to believe that if it weren't for women, there would not be a market for cars with navigation devices.

On *Are You Smarter Than a Fifth Grader*, Jeff Foxworthy asked, "Who was the first American astronaut to orbit the earth?"

The contestant answered correctly, "John Glenn."

Mr. Foxworthy quipped, "Did you know that he orbited three times, and the reason he did ... because like most men, he didn't check his map?"

A financial plan is a must in order to help us map a destination, navigate the rough waters that will happen, and stay the course. You may be saying, "Okay, David, you made your point. We know that we need to plan. Where do we go from here?"

Here are the steps:

1. Set your goals. Ask yourself what type of lifestyle you want to maintain and how much income you need to maintain it. What are your irregular expenses (buying a new car every certain number of years, grandchildren's cost of education, household goods, vacations, etc.)? List any other financial goals.

2. Decide whether you want to hire an adviser or try to go it alone.

3. Once you have chosen an adviser, you will need to invest some time in building a plan. You may need to meet with your adviser several times. This is not a process of mechanically inputting data in a spreadsheet and waiting for a plan to pop out. Many times, the plan needs to be modified until it is the right fit. You will know when the plan is correct for you. Everyone's situation is different, and this is a very personal process.

I thoroughly enjoy this part of working with clients; it gives them time to focus on themselves and their needs. I don't know about you, but I enjoy talking about myself on occasion. (My family is probably saying, "What do you mean on occasion? How about all of the time?"). This is time for my clients to talk about what is important to them.

If your objective is for you and your spouse to navigate the retirement waters together, you will both need to attend the meetings. Done individually, the result can create discord. Even if one spouse makes the decisions, they both need to be involved. An exception is when one spouse suffers from dementia or a form of dementia. Each person's concerns, needs, and desires should be equally respected.

Many people do not think about the vulnerability of a surviving spouse when one of them passes away, but a grieving person can be targeted by predators. Also, they are susceptible to making bad decisions. When couples plan together, they have peace of mind in knowing when one of them passes away, the surviving spouse has the security of a trusted and respectful relationship, assuming you are working with the right advisers. You know your spouse will be cared for by someone who cares for them. In addition, the surviving spouse will have a road map that both spouses helped put together.

o   Make sure your plan addresses all the risks associated with living longer:
o   If either or both of you should need long-term care, what is your financial risk exposure?
o   If you do have financial risk, what is the most efficient and cost-effective way to reduce or eliminate the risk?
o   If you need long-term-care insurance, make sure it is customized to your plan.

o   Do you and your spouse have enough money to maintain purchasing power throughout your life expectancy?

o   What are the smart investment choices you need to make?

o   Is your money positioned correctly?

o   Are you paying more in taxes than the government requires? Which assets should you use first to create income?

Have your plan reviewed annually to keep things up to date and to modify where necessary.

For those of you saying, "I know this is important if I am to achieve my goal to live with independence and dignity in my remaining years, but I can't find time to plan right now." If that is you, I will leave you with this: most of us have probably heard the story about a man who wanted to quit procrastinating. Motivated, he signed up to take a class called Procrastinators Anonymous. He was never able to attend because every time the man showed up for the meeting, there was a sign on the door: "Meeting moved to next week at the same time."

Opting to put off today for what we can do tomorrow is easy for all of us. In *The Total Money Makeover,* Dave Ramsey warns us not to believe the myth: "I don't have time to work on a budget, retirement plan, or estate plan. The truth is you don't have time not to." Knowing what you now know to protect yourself in retirement will not do you one ounce of good if you don't take action.

A client who had put off planning recently told me she can sleep better and enjoy life now because of planning. Another client was walking blindly into the future, not knowing what could rob her of her independence. People are frequently astonished at the peace of mind planning gives them. Many didn't plan because they were afraid of what they might find out. Like almost anything in life, fear can hold us back, cripple us, and keep us from doing what we know we should. Dale Carnegie said, "Inaction breeds doubt and fear. Action breeds confidence and courage. If you want to conquer fear, do not sit home and think about it. Go out and get busy."

We can certainly apply Mr. Carnegie's wisdom to financial planning. We need to get busy. Who doesn't want to control fear instead of letting fear control us? Who doesn't want to have more confidence? As the famous Nike slogan says, "Just do it." If you don't do it for you, do it for those you love. May God bless your efforts.

CHAPTER 9

Conclusion

I hope you have found this book helpful. I'm confident it gives you the information you need whether you're preplanning to protect your assets from the high cost of long-term care or if you have a loved one in a facility. If you currently have a loved one in a long-term-care facility, which is called crisis planning, you now have the tools to help protect their life savings.

With ten thousand baby boomers retiring daily, preplanning for the cost of long-term care is critical. If left out of your retirement plan, you're not addressing the number one reason why people go broke in retirement. The good news is protecting your assets is relatively easy. You simply shift the money you're not using to protect the money you are using. By changing the position of your assets, you can add thousands of extra dollars to pay for care if you should need it. In addition, you can provide a death benefit if you use a portion of the money for care or none of it. Depending on which preplanning strategy you use, the death benefit may be income tax-free to your loved ones. Most important, you will be providing a layer of security while staying in control of the money. It is simply a left pocket to right pocket plan of action.

Once you get the long-term-care elephant out of the room, you will have greater peace of mind. You will have helped eliminate one of retirees' two greatest fears: "What if I need health care in the future? What will happen to my savings?" The high cost of care affects seniors' second fear: running out of money. When you address protecting your savings in case of needing care, you have taken a positive step in maintaining your security, independence, and dignity.

Regarding independence, in order to receive Medicaid benefits, in some states, you have to be in a facility. Preplanning allows you to dictate your care needs and desires. People I have talked to only want to go to a nursing home if they have to. I feel the same way. Planning ahead of time can allow you to stay home as long as possible. Although in-home care is less costly than nursing home care, 24-7 in-home care is difficult for most families to afford to pay privately. In Oregon, 24-7 care averages $16,104 per month even if there is no in-home medical care required.

When a spouse needs care and there's a married couple involved, almost all—if not all—of their assets can be protected. They don't need to spend down their savings to qualify for Medicaid benefits. In the case of a single person, some or most of their savings can be protected. The misinformation that a single person has to spend down to

$2,000 before they can receive Medicaid benefits is simply not true. Don't let anyone tell you otherwise—even if they are a professional.

As of the writing of this book, Medicaid benefits are still available, but no one knows for how long. If you need Medicaid-planning advice, reach out to someone who is a specialist. Check out references, experience, and credentials.

o   If you received a $100,000 bill a year that was not part of your retirement plan, what would you do?
o   What are your objections to buying long-term-care insurance even if you don't use it you don't lose it and you remain in control of the money?
o   What would motivate you to buy insurance to protect your assets, dignity, and independence?
o   Do you have a plan if a health situation threatened your security?
o   What if Medicaid is no longer available and you do not have insurance or enough savings to private pay and you or your spouse needs care? What would you do?

If the husband doesn't see the need to insure against long-term care for himself, he should be compassionate about his wife's benefit and consider insurance for her. Statistics show that when a man needs care, the wife becomes the caregiver until she no longer can. Men pass before their wives do. What about the caregiving spouse? What if she needs care in the future? Who's going to step up for her quality of life? I have found parents do not want to be a burden on their children. They want to remain independent.

The government has given us tax-free long-term-care options through the Pension Protection Act (PPA). All you have to do is take advantage of them by taking out a PPA-filed life insurance policy with a long-term-care rider or an annuity with the same type of rider. This can help protect your assets, allow you to stay home longer, give you tax-free money for care costs, and significantly leverage your savings.

Annuities can help with the number two fear of retirees: running out of money. By putting guaranteed income payments on a monthly basis in place—and creating your own defined benefit program—this strategy is chosen by 60 percent of those who learn about it. Most people don't know this program is available.

There are about $2 trillion in deferred annuities, and most are owned by seniors. While these provide tax-free deferral and a competitive interest rate, they do nothing to protect assets once long-term care is needed. There are also tax-deferred annuities with the same benefits and asset protection, but 98 percent of insurance companies don't provide this annuity benefit.

The annuity grows tax deferred as any tax-deferred annuity does, but if long-term care is needed, it can be converted to a Medicaid Compliant Annuity that meets the Medicaid rules. The advantage to this approach is it is all done internally with the insurance company. If you have an annuity with another company and need a Medicaid-compliant annuity to get a loved one Medicaid qualified, you can move your annuity to a Medicaid Compliant Annuity, which can be done tax-free through a 1035 exchange or a trustee-to-trustee transfer. If it is still in the surrender-charge phase, it can cost you to make the transfer.

That is not the case if you have your deferred annuity with a company that can provide this benefit internally. No surrender charge is applied even during the surrender-charge period. What you end up with is all the benefits of tax deferral, a competitive interest rate, and an asset-protection strategy. You have all your bases covered. This works under current Medicaid rules, but if the annuity rules or Medicaid is eliminated, this strategy would not apply.

I hope you use this book as a reference. If I can help you, contact me at david@almond-financial.com. My website is almond-financial.com.

Planning for long-term care has never been more important. A passion of mine is saying, "Don't go broke— and then on Medicaid. Have your savings protected so you have quality of life. And don't be a victim of misinformation."

I hope your money lasts a lifetime and that you have the peace of mind to know your hard-earned savings are protected from the high cost of long-term care.

My best,

David Almond

ABOUT THE AUTHOR

 David L. Almond has been a certified financial planner since 1989 and has a master's degree in financial services. He is a past long-term-care instructor for the state of Washington and served on the board of directors for Baptist Manor, a Portland, Oregon, nursing facility. He is contributing author of *Age without Rage* and is the author of *The Seven Steps to a Worry-Free Retirement*.

Over the past eighteen years, David has dedicated his practice to long-term-care crisis planning and preplanning. His passion is helping those currently in care facilities and others who want to protect their savings from the high cost of care. Ken Dychtwald, PhD, the leading authority on aging in America, said, "David Almond's experience and knowledge of the risks that retirees now face is unique."

David can be reached at david@almond-financial .com along with his website www.almond-financial.com.

Printed in the United States
By Bookmasters